An Introduction to

The

OLD TESTAMENT
TEMPLATE

LANDA COPE

AN INTRODUCTION TO

OLD TESTAMENT
TEMPLATE

REDISCOVERING GOD'S PRINCIPLES
FOR DISCIPLING NATIONS

SECOND EDITION

YWAM PUBLISHING
Seattle, Washington

YWAM Publishing is the publishing ministry of Youth With A Mission. Youth With A Mission (YWAM) is an international missionary organization of Christians from many denominations dedicated to presenting Jesus Christ to this generation. To this end, YWAM has focused its efforts in three main areas: (1) training and equipping believers for their part in fulfilling the Great Commission (Matthew 28:19), (2) personal evangelism, and (3) mercy ministry (medical and relief work).

For a free catalog of books and materials, call (425) 771-1153 or (800) 922-2143. Visit us online at www.ywampublishing.com.

An Introduction to the Old Testament Template:
Rediscovering God's Principles for Discipling Nations
Copyright © 2006, 2011 by Landa Lea Cope
Second Edition

Published by YWAM Publishing
a ministry of Youth With A Mission
P.O. Box 55787, Seattle, WA 98155

First printing 2011

First edition published in 2006 by The Template Institute Press, 1268 Burtigny, Switzerland. All rights reserved. For more information visit www.templateinstitute.com.

Library of Congress Cataloging-in-Publication Data
Cope, Landa L.
    An Introduction to the Old Testament template : rediscovering God's principles for discipling nations / Landa L. Cope. — 2nd ed.
        p. cm.
    Includes bibliographical references.
    ISBN 978-1-57658-560-3
    1. Christian life—Biblical teaching. 2. Discipling (Christianity)—Biblical teaching. I. Title.
    BS1199.C43C67 2011
    248—dc22   2011003253

Printed in the United States of America

To my mom, who, with all her highs and lows, never wavered from her love and commitment to the truth and power of the Word of God. The desperate prayers of a loving mother are not wasted.

Margaret Adeline Kelley Cope, 1912–2002

CONTENTS

PART III: IF WE ARE GOING TO DISCIPLE ALL NATIONS

Acknowledgments

There are so many people to thank that I am sure I will unintentionally miss some. Please forgive me. Any work we produce is really the sum total of all that others have given us and the grace of God to help us use it.

I am grateful to Loren Cunningham and Tom Marshall for sparking a burning passion for God's kingdom truth in my heart. Joy Dawson, Campbell McAlpine, and Gordon Olsen modeled careful, methodical passion for the Word of God as a foundation for everything we do. Michael Cassidy was and is my hero who has let his heart be broken with the lost truths of God and the impact this has had on our nations. Gunnar Olson listened to my cassette of the first message and opened up doors for me to share Christ around the world. And there are scores of pastors and biblical scholars all over the world who have assured me that I was not crazy and that this message must get out.

On the working team I need to mention the Omaha ladies edit team, who got me through the first draft; my P.A. Erin Pennington, Jenni Lotz, and Olivia Jackson, who looked up loads of facts; John Darnall, Chris Ruzin, and Cameron Thorp, who got us through the artwork, website, and logo design; Erin Pennington and Tove Poulsen, who gave the energy and commitment to push through the last drafts; and, of course, Lucile Allen, who made it all so much more readable with her final editing.

Many thanks go to ten years of Advanced Principles of Communications students who helped hammer out the ideas and multiply the message. I could not have continued without your steady encouragement that this was life-changing stuff. And the same with the thousands of people who have attended seminars around the world and given feedback. Larry Wright and his team at Procla-Media caught the vision very early on and produced a really good video series that has blessed, and is blessing, thousands with this material.

To my dear friends Fiona, Colleen, Matt, Tove, and Erin for believing in the material as much as I do and never letting me forget that God is near. And to my team at Burtigny who have given me so much grace and encouragement to do this work while they carried other weights in my absence.

Finally, and always, my thanks to God, who lets me continue to enter into the ecstasy of knowing him and talking about him all over the world.

Foreword

In a small cabin on the western slopes of Colorado in August of 1975, our family of four was taking a holiday week. On the second day I received in prayer from the Lord seven "spheres of society" to be used strategically to disciple nations (Matthew 28:18–20). I wrote them on a yellow legal pad: family (home); church (religion); education; media (electronic and printed); celebration (arts, entertainment, and sports); economy (commerce, including research and development, production, and sales and service); and government (all branches).

The next day my wife, Darlene, and I were invited to meet with Bill and Vonette Bright, founders of Campus Crusade for Christ, as they too were in Colorado. As we visited, I was reaching into my coat pocket for my list when Bill announced to us that God had shown him the strategy for discipling a nation! I looked at his list, and they included the same areas.

This is not new, but a renewed revelation. In the nineteenth century Abraham Kuyper of Holland had a list of four "jurisdictions" from God through his Word. William Carey, a London shoe cobbler who became a pioneer missionary in India, launched programs in all seven spheres of society. He published the first periodical in all of Asia, founded a lending bank for the poor, started schools, planted churches, and helped change laws to stop widow burning, to name a few.

The truths of God's Word remain true in all centuries. The transformation of nations through transformed followers of Jesus can and will happen in this, the twenty-first, century as we apply his truth in and through our lives.

Heads of state, corporation CEOs, church leaders, and leaders of all spheres of society have been impacted and encouraged by Landa Cope's presentation of God's template for transforming nations. Although she arranges the spheres a little differently than I do, the principles and strategy are the same.

I'm happy that Landa, a friend of more than three decades, has put this powerful truth into writing. Read and be challenged—and changed.

Loren Cunningham
Kailua-Kona, Hawaii
November 2005

FOREWORD

Landa Cope is both a prophetess and an Esther for such a time as this. Of all the speakers and leaders I have known around the world over the last couple of decades, no one quite matches Landa for her passion to see nations discover the divine pattern of living. Some people think *individual,* others think *local church,* but Landa thinks *nation.* In fact, she thinks *the world.* But she sees the world through the lens of God's purposes for the multiple nations of the world.

And because there are so few Christian leaders in the world who deeply think nationally, Landa has special significance and this book is of particular importance, especially for Christian leaders, whether they operate from a local church, parachurch, or denominational base.

In this volume Landa is challenging all of us to think afresh about what sort of God we really have. Is he concerned simply with the things of heaven and how to get his sinful earthlings there? Of course, that is major in the divine intention, and no one knows that better than Landa. But she has also profoundly grasped God's Old Testament word: "I am the LORD who practices steadfast love, justice, and righteousness *in the earth.* For in these things I delight, declares the LORD" (Jeremiah 9:24 ESV, emphasis added). This scripture gives us the breathtaking affirmation that not only is the Lord himself a God of unswerving love, justice, and righteousness, this being his fundamental character, but he actually *practices* them. He works them out in deeds. That is the kind of God he is. That is his character. He is an active, working, functioning God, caught up in certain divine deeds and practice.

But now, fasten your seat belts for the next bit—and this is what Landa has grasped way better than most people I know—this God works out his characteristics and practices them not simply in heaven but on earth. This ties in with Jesus' instruction to us to pray for the kingdom to come and for his will to be done on earth as it is in heaven (Matthew 6:10). And it also fits in with both the Psalmist's and St. Paul's reminder to us that "the earth is the LORD's" (Psalm 24:1; 1 Corinthians 10:26). So the earth is God's special arena for practicing and working out his love, justice, and righteousness.

And the arena in which this is especially meant to be worked out is individual nations. Landa's powerful and prophetic volume is therefore a passionate appeal to the Lord's people to join in the study and search for God's nation-building values. My prayer is that this book will be used and read widely and that we will catch something of Landa's panoramic vision, be challenged by some of her encyclopedic grasp of this theme, and be volitionally motivated to discover afresh the real biblical strategies needed under God to bring changes he wants to see in his world.

Absorbing this volume will put a bomb under our seats and catapult us out into the world with new insight, energy, wisdom, and effective transformational ministries.

If you are ready and have the stomach and heart for such a challenge, read on. But if you are overly devoted to the armchair, then put this book on one side, relax back into your comfort zone, and miss out on one of the greatest adventures life and eternity can offer. Because winning and truly discipling the nations is just that kind of adventure.

Michael Cassidy
South Africa

PREFACE

I am sitting in a small guest house in Potchefstroom, South Africa. Last night, and the two nights before, I spoke to a thousand South African university students about the call of God on each of their lives to bless and develop their nation. As I worshiped with them— and it was powerful worship—I was reminded of the summer of 1972 at the Munich Olympics. A thousand young people gathered in a tent just outside the city. We were there for the first-ever Olympic outreach, and we were there to change our world. Joy Dawson spoke on "God Is Always Greater."

From that one outreach and Youth With A Mission's one base in Lausanne, Switzerland, our mission exploded to over a thousand bases in 150 countries and hundreds of outreaches all over the world, involving millions of young people over the next thirty-three years. YWAM, Operation Mobilization (OM), Campus Crusade, and other Spirit-led youth missions launched what missiologists now refer to as the third wave of missions. Faithful, amazing God!

Now it is time for the fourth wave! It is time for the largest church in history to become the deepest church in history. Last night, speaking to those South African students, I saw the face of the future. Pray with me for the release of this new generation of world-changers. Pray with me for a global revolution of political and economic justice, revival of the church, and explosion of wholeness in individuals and families. Pray with me that God's glory will be seen, and that every Christian worldwide will follow Saint Francis of Assisi's admonition to be a witness all day, every day—and to use words when necessary.

God never changes. Pray that we, his people, do.

Landa Lea Cope
Potchefstroom, South Africa

Part I

The Journey

INTRODUCTION

This book is dedicated to the study of what the Bible has to say about all of life, including government, family, the arts, education, science, communication, economics, and the church. I and those who have contributed to this book want to rediscover a faith that influences our thinking and actions in every arena of living.

In history Christians thought and acted in ways that influenced the communities and nations in which they lived. Much of that influence had a positive effect on things like public education, workers' rights, economic development, the concept of a free press, and help for the victimized and disenfranchised. We believe that this kind of influence is lacking in Christian life today, and we would like to discover why.

Martin Luther is noted as having said that a gospel that does not deal with the issues of the day is not the gospel at all. We want to discover the biblical thinking that will address the issues of the twenty-first century in an effective and redemptive way. There is a reason the Christian faith has become weak and ineffectual in dealing with issues of politics, economics, beauty, the family, and daily life. We want to discover what has gone wrong, but more importantly we want to rediscover the biblical basis that led generations of believers to influence their times.

We are searching, and I invite you to join the search. I have put the challenge of these questions to presidents, members of cabinets, and leaders in politics, business, and church on every continent of the world. It is striking a chord of need. We have begun this work to get the message out and bring multinational, multicultural thinking and faith to the process. Our goal is to help bring vital, relevant, effective Christian thought and action back into the twenty-first century. We are on a journey with more questions than answers; I invite your companionship and contribution.

CHAPTER 1

WHAT'S WRONG WITH THIS PICTURE?

Do you have eyes but fail to see, and ears but fail to hear?
MARK 8:18

Once more Jesus put his hands on the man's eyes. Then his eyes were opened, his sight was restored, and he saw everything clearly.
MARK 8:25

I was mindlessly channel surfing through scores of TV programs to pass the time. I landed on a British journalist who was saying that Christians believe that if many of them live in a community, it will affect that community for good. The greater the Christian presence, the greater the benefit to the society at large. I agreed with the commentator; that is what we teach.

He then proposed to look at the most Christianized city in America to see how this influence works out practically. He defined "Christianized" as the community with the largest percentage of believers regularly attending church. This, I thought, was a good conservative working definition of "Christianized."

By that definition, then, Dallas, Texas, was the most Christianized city in America at that time. More people per capita attended church on any given Sunday than any other community in the country. Churches abound in Dallas, and a large number boast full pews. Our journalist proposed to look at the social demographics of Dallas to see how this "Christian blessing" worked out within that community.

He looked at statistics and studies on crime, safety on the streets, police enforcement, and the justice and penal system. He looked at health care, hospitals, emergency care, contagious diseases, the infant mortality rate, and the distribution of caregivers. He reviewed education—equality of schools, safety, test scores, and graduation statistics. Jobs, housing, and general economics were evaluated. Can you get a job? Can you get housing? Does potential income match available housing? He looked at homelessness and at programs for those unable to care for themselves. Is there equality regardless of color, creed, or income? And so on. Each of these categories was evaluated according to racial and economic factors.

The TV host looked at the statistics and information you would be concerned about if you were going to raise your children in a community. Will my children be safe on the streets and at school? Can they get a respectable education? Will I be able to house, clothe, and feed my family? Will my children have blatant exposure to drugs and other destructive influences? Can my family be protected from disease? Is adequate medical care available if they get sick? Can I get legal help and fairness in the judicial system? Are the police interested in our protection? And is all of this true regardless of my color, nationality, or creed?

About an hour of the program went by, and I was watching it alone. By the time my British host was done with the Dallas study, I was devastated. No one would want to live in a city in that condition. The crime, the decrepit social systems, the disease, the economic discrepancies, the racial injustice all disqualified this community from having an adequate quality of life. And this was the "most Christianized" city in America. I wanted to weep.

The program was not finished. The host took this devastating picture of a broken community to the Christian leaders and asked for their observations. He chose pastors of status and integrity, the kind of pastors Christians would respect. One by one, each pastor viewed the same facts that I had just seen about the condition of the city. With simplicity the narrator asked, "As a Christian leader, what is your response to the condition of your community?" Without exception, in various ways, they all said the same thing: "This is not my concern. I'm a spiritual leader."

The program finished, the room was silent, and my world began to crumble. Many years of my work as a missionary have been spent addressing Christianity's critics, specifically those in the media. (This is not generally very difficult, as their accusations are often ill-informed or poorly formulated.) But if this journalist had turned the microphone to me for comment at the closing of his program, I would have been speechless. I was shocked to silence—by the facts.

I had no argument against the case this journalist had built. As Christians, we do say our faith, lived out, will influence a society toward good. We go beyond this. I have heard it said, and have taught, that it only takes 20 percent of a society believing anything to influence, even lead, the other 80 percent in a given direction. We teach that the gospel is good for society, that its values will bless those beyond the members of faith. But the facts about Dallas did not support this claim. We must look at the facts! Dallas had considerably more than 20 percent professing Christians. Could we say that this city is the legacy of Christian influence?

I was reeling with implications and questions. Why had I not been honest enough to see the discrepancy between my teaching and the visible results? Why had it taken a non-Christian to point these things out to me? How could we Christian leaders say "quality of life" issues are not our concern? If the gospel does influence all of society, how could America, with 78 percent of people identifying as Christian, be slipping from biblical values in so many arenas?[1]

Slipping in justice, health care, and literacy? Slipping into crime, immorality, poverty, corruption, drug addiction, homelessness, and more? How was it that I, and the myriad committed Christians I knew, had never realized this? Why had we not judged ourselves—and found ourselves wanting?

SEARCH FOR TRUTH

I came to Christianity reluctantly. As a college student I was a committed atheist, giving speeches on why not to believe in the Bible. I longed for truth, practical truth, that could be lived on a daily basis. I hoped for a truth that could lead to justice and genuine love for others. I converted to Christianity because I became convinced that it was the only belief system that explains the reality of the universe we live in, good and bad. My encounter with that truth, and with the person of Jesus Christ, catapulted me into the kingdom of God. I have since spent my years trying to learn more of the truths of the kingdom and how to live them out practically in my daily life and work. Nevertheless, I have always said that if it could be proven to me that the teachings of the Bible and the life of Christ were not true, I would reevaluate everything I believe. Nothing had ever shaken my confidence in Christianity more than this television program. Now my feet were to the fire.

As I battled with the questions this program's revelations demanded, I could see at least three possible answers:

1. God does not exist.
2. God and/or God's Word are not true. The Bible does teach that its values applied will influence society at large, but practically it does not work.
3. Christians today are not applying biblical values, and therefore we do not see the influence those truths should have in our world and have had in history.

In my heart I knew that the third option had to be the case. I have never been a Christian for primarily historical, emotional, or personal reasons. I am a follower of Christ because I believe the Bible is true and that whenever its teaching and principles are measured and applied, they will prove true. My faith was on the line, and I believed that the God I knew was up to the challenge. But I needed answers!

Early in my journey with Christ I discovered that some questions are too big for our pitifully limited minds. I learned that these questions are not too great for God. He delights to reveal himself and lead us to understanding, but he must do the revealing. For overwhelming questions, I have a special shelf in the back of my mind. We are not to throw out the great and crushing questions that challenge our faith and the very nature and character of the One in whom we believe. If we do not face them, we lose the opportunity for God to reveal himself in a greater way. But we cannot wrestle with life's most serious dilemmas by ourselves; we do not have the understanding. We must hold these painful issues before the throne of God. In so doing, we grow in the knowledge of God.

These pressing observations, prompted by the honest analysis of a British journalist, question the validity of what Christians say about the influence of Christianity in a community. What we teach does not match the real impact of Christianity today. I put these agonizing questions on the shelf with a prayer. "Father, I believe your Word, and I believe you when you say that you want to bless all peoples and use the church to do it. I believe that your principles are true. But, Lord, we do not have the influence we should have in our day. Why, Lord? Help me understand. Help me see." And he did!

TRIP TO AFRICA

I began my overseas life in North Africa—four wonderful years in the land of the pharaohs. I loved Egypt and would gladly have spent my entire life there. More than twenty years later, within months of watching the Dallas documentary, I was on my way to a more expansive exploratory trip of the African continent. For two months I traversed from western to eastern to southern Africa. I spent hours in airplanes looking down on Africa's vastness. The "Dallas questions" still sat on my mental back shelf. How could a Christian community be in such abominable shape? How could the gospel result in such chaos?

As I visited primarily Christianized nations—Togo, Ghana, Nigeria, Kenya, Uganda, and South Africa—my anguish increased. Missions statistics that I had quoted with joy burned in my mind. "Africa, 80 percent Christian south of the Sahara by the end of the twentieth century." "Africa, the most evangelized continent in the world." "Africa, the most churched continent by the end of this century." In each nation the story was the same. Poverty, disease, violence, corruption, injustice, and chaos met me at every turn. I found myself asking, Is this "Thy kingdom come, Thy will be done in earth, as it is in heaven"?[2] Is this what the blessing of the gospel brought into a community looks like? Is this what a nation looks like when it is "reached"? In southern Africa nearly every person has heard the gospel. Churches are planted and full. African evangelists abound and continue the work. Is this what it looks like when our work as Christians is finished in a nation? God forbid! My anguish increased.

You may say, "This is unfair. These were poor countries before the gospel came!" You are right, but some are poorer and more diseased now, *after* the gospel has come. I spent many hours asking God how this could be. How could we as Christians, and especially missionaries, be patting our backs for a job well done in southern and central Africa? How could we speak so glowingly of the gospel's great reformation of Europe and North America and not see that none of that nation-changing reality is being experienced in Africa? How could anyone believe that this devastated Africa is "finished"? How could anyone believe that Africa—or deteriorating Dallas, for that matter—is an example of the impact of Christianity? How could we hold up the condition of so-called Christianized nations today as a trophy of the truth, as proof that where the gospel of Jesus Christ is spread, blessing accompanies it?

My heart was heavy as I traveled Africa, as I thought about my own nation. My prayer became, "Lord, what has gone wrong?" Nearly two hundred years of concentrated missions effort on Africa—how could it result in this? With a dawning revelation that would change my understanding of missions and my life calling, God spoke simply and fundamentally: "The devastation you see is the fruit of preaching salvation alone, without the rest of the biblical message."

CHAPTER 2

WE'VE LOST OUR
CHRISTIAN MINDS

Jesus replied: "'Love the Lord your God with all your heart and
with all your soul and with all your mind.' This is the first and the
greatest commandment."
MATTHEW 22:37–38

"For if I pray in a tongue, my spirit prays, but my mind is
unfruitful. So what shall I do? I will pray with my spirit, but I will
also pray with my mind."
1 CORINTHIANS 14:14–15

Salvation? What could possibly be the problem with preaching
salvation?" you may ask. The answer to that? Nothing! There
is nothing wrong with the *salvation* part of the gospel message we
preach today. But we evangelicals talk about the salvation message
as though the initial experience of salvation (i.e., conversion, being
born again) is the *only* message. Jesus preached that the only way to
enter the kingdom of heaven is through him, but he constantly put
salvation in the context of the broader message of the kingdom of

heaven. He never referred to the *gospel of salvation*. He taught the *gospel of the kingdom*, which includes salvation and the truth about every dimension of life. Yet more than 150 years of mission work has been dominated by this concept of "being saved" as the singular goal.

The result of this truncated gospel message is no less tragic than a grown child still incapable of doing anything for himself or herself. Something has gone terribly wrong. God's design has been interrupted, and this life has not fully developed. The child is still precious and a great gift of life, but God's plans and purposes for that person have been distorted. That principle is the same in all of his kingdom. We are not only to be born again; we are also to mature in the ways of God in all parts of life. We are meant to have our minds transformed and every thought taken captive with the truths of God's great kingdom. We are to know how God wants us to live!

In what Michael Cassidy of South Africa calls "the Great Reversal,"[1] we have taken the holistic message of the Old and New Testaments and reduced it to the entry point into the kingdom. The beginning has become the goal: conversion. We want to "get people saved." When we get them saved, we want to "get them in church." We then move on to reach those who have never heard. This is our concept of missions; this is evangelism. When a people has heard our gospel of salvation and the church is planted, we believe we have finished our job. But two, three, four hundred years ago, church leaders would have found this emphasis on salvation, to the exclusion of the rest of the message, astounding. The message that reformed Western cultures and built nations on solidly Christian values was not the gospel of salvation but the gospel of the kingdom.

The truths of the gospel of the kingdom are transformative. They teach us how to live every part of life. Our transformed lives are to be salt and light to our families, neighborhoods, communities, and nations, making them *better* places to live. Not perfect communities, not heaven on earth, but better because the influence of good is as great, if not greater, than evil. It has been said that no revivalist in church history believed that God's purpose ended with revival. Each believed that true revival culminated in significant reformation of communities through the transformed church's influence on society at large.

The early church transformed Israel, revolutionized the Roman Empire, and laid foundations for Western European nations to become the most prosperous in the world. What a different impact we see in modern mission history. Evangelized Africa is worse today in disease, crime, justice, economics, and the family than before Christianity came to the continent.[2] America has a huge percentage of practicing believers, and yet it also is decreasing in moral fiber and quality of life in every category. Missionaries in the subcontinent of India say that while we quote that Nagaland is 80 percent Christianized, we fail to note that 70 percent of the teenagers in the capital city are drug addicts. Rwanda, with some sixty years of ongoing revival in the church, suffers genocide in tribal civil war. Some say that there are more Christians alive today than the sum total of Christians in history. Where is the power to influence and transform communities that the apostle Paul, Saint Patrick, John Calvin, and many others experienced in their day?

Does the fruit of modern evangelism today reflect "Thy kingdom come, Thy will be done in earth, as it in heaven"? Surely not! So, where have we gone wrong? How did we come to such a reduced gospel?

THE SPLIT CHRISTIAN MIND

Over the past two centuries Christians, especially evangelicals, have developed a split view of the world that dominates much of church today. This dualistic thinking developed as one part of the church took the stand that God was responsible for salvation and that it was the church's responsibility to look after people's basic needs, such as food, clothing, shelter, health, and education. Another part of the church responded to this stance with a resounding "No!" This group believed that only people's souls were of value and that the church was to focus on evangelism. This latter group, identified as *evangelicals,* was concerned with "spiritual" or "sacred" matters, while the former group, identified as *liberals,* was concerned with "material" or "secular" matters. This split sacred-secular view of the world was exaggerated by an increasing emphasis among some evangelicals on the immediate return of Christ and the belief that the material world would be destroyed.

The split gospel looks like this:

spiritual	material
evangelical	liberal
salvation	social action
eternal	temporal
heavenly	earthly
sacred	secular

This, of course, is a very basic way of looking at considerably more complex doctrinal issues. I am neither a theologian nor a historian, and I am not attempting to deal with these broader issues. My point here is simply to show that a dualistic view of the world entered the thinking of the church, and this view reduced the gospel preached by many today to salvation alone. Many Christians became solely concerned about the invisible issues of the faith: salvation, prayer, spiritual warfare, heaven, and healing. We began to believe we only had time to get souls saved.

The tragedy in this division, as is so often the case, is that both sides were right and both sides were wrong. Evangelicals were right about what the gospel *is* concerned with and wrong in what they felt was *not* the gospel's concern. The gospel of the kingdom that Jesus taught, built on the entire teaching of God to Israel through Moses and the prophets, was a message that dealt with sin and salvation, with heaven and hell, with prayer and spiritual warfare. The liberals were accurate in that the gospel is also a message of God's desire for justice in government, equity in economics, righteousness in science and technology, freedom and honesty in communication, strength in family, and beauty and truth in the arts.

The result of a diminished and split gospel is clear in the world we live in today. Never have there been more Christians, in more churches, in more nations, speaking more languages of the world. But I think it is also fair to say that never has the spread of the church had less impact in communities. The church today is widespread, but it is also weak, because we have lost most of the gospel message. With our split view of the world, we say that the social, economic, and judicial issues of our communities are not our concern. We say we are "spiritual leaders" and do not need to worry about "secular" matters.

While we do not need to stop preaching the message of salvation, we desperately need to regain the rest of the truths of God's kingdom. We need to renew our Christian minds to see our lives transformed. We need to conform every thought to the thinking of Christ. Then the twenty-first century church will turn our world upside down. Then the body of Christ will not only be large and diverse, but it will regain its power of influence.

CHAPTER 3

WE'VE LOST OUR MISSION

For if he lays the foundation and is not able to finish it, everyone who sees it will ridicule him, saying, "This fellow began to build and was not able to finish."
LUKE 14:29–30

Perseverance must finish its work so that you may be mature and complete, not lacking anything.
JAMES 1:4

A friend taught me an important lesson. When given a new job to do, always ask, "What does a job well done look like?" You cannot possibly do well what you do not understand. If the church is to do what Christ intended us to do, we must understand what our job is and what it is to look like when we have finished.

Toward the end of his life Jesus prayed, "[Father,] I have brought you glory on earth by completing the work you gave me to do."[1] His Father had sent him into time and space to accomplish specific objectives. He knew what they were, and he completed them. The work of reaching the entire world was not accomplished at his death, but Jesus understood that he was not sent to do everything. Much of the Father's mission would be carried on and completed by the church that Jesus would leave behind. But, for the time being, Jesus' specific job on earth as Messiah was complete.

After nearly thirty years in missions, I marvel at this text. So often as Christian workers we do not even know what our job is. If something needs to be done, we assume it must be our responsibility to do it. I don't ever remember hearing a minister say, "I completed my work." Jesus, however, did not think that *everything* was his responsibility. He knew what the Father had sent him to do, and he knew when he had completed it. We can learn much from this in our own lives and callings. What has God called *us* to do?

Another thing that strikes me in this text is that the Father was glorified because Jesus finished his job. When I am introduced as a speaker, my hosts often string together a list of accomplishments from my life. They are trying to give the audience a point of reference and reasons why they might want to listen to me. While I appreciate that, it is important that I do not become impressed with myself. God is not looking at the past; he is looking at the finish. He is challenging me not only to begin well but to finish well. Then, and only then, will he be glorified in my life and through my work. These are sobering challenges and good questions to raise in prayer on a regular basis. Am I doing what God called me to do? Will I finish it?

WHAT IS THE WORK OF THE CHURCH?

We can apply these questions to the institution of the church. What is the work of the church? How do we know if we have finished it? How do we evaluate and measure a generation's obedience as the body of Christ? What are our specific goals, and how do we develop strategies and evaluate their value? Answering these questions is key to transforming a huge church into an influential church in the twenty-first century. Throughout history some have said our work is to get people saved and to build the church globally. Others have said we are to provide people's material needs such as food, shelter, and protection. But what does God say? What does the Bible teach as the mandate for our existence on this planet? If we know what God's Word says, we can build our future on solid foundations.

At the end of his life on earth Jesus gave instructions to his disciples. This is the disciples' record of what he said:

Matthew 28:18–20

Then Jesus came to them and said, "All authority in heaven and on earth has been given to me. Therefore go and make disciples of all nations, baptizing them in the name of the Father and of the Son and of the Holy Spirit, and teaching them to obey everything I have commanded you. And surely I am with you always, to the very end of the age."

Mark 16:15

He said to them, "Go into all the world and preach the good news to all creation."

Luke 24:45–47

Then he opened their minds so they could understand the Scriptures. He told them, "This is what is written: The Christ will suffer and rise from the dead on the third day, and repentance and forgiveness of sins will be preached in his name to all nations, beginning at Jerusalem."

Many have reduced these objectives to two simple mandates: Christ has called us to "reach every creature" and to "disciple all nations." This fits with God's emphasis throughout the Bible for humanity's very existence. There is a continuity from Adam to Christ, a golden thread of purpose for our existence. To Adam and Eve, male and female, God speaks these words:

Genesis 1:28

God blessed them and said to them, "Be fruitful and increase in number; fill the earth and subdue it. Rule over the fish of the sea and the birds of the air and over every living creature that moves on the ground."

To Abraham and his descendants God spoke time and again, repeating the following:

Genesis 22:17–18

"I will surely bless you and make your descendants as numerous as the stars in the sky and as the sand on the seashore. Your descendants will take possession of the cities of their enemies, and through your offspring all nations on earth will be blessed, because you have obeyed me."

This emphasis on multiplying and blessing, the quantitative and qualitative aspects, was in God's purpose and plan for humans from creation. We are here to fill the earth and steward it to God's glory. This purpose did not disappear or dissipate with the fall of man and the coming of sin, although sin would now have to be dealt with.

Therefore we can look at the work of the church in two dimensions: the breadth (the quantitative task of reaching every creature) and the depth (the qualitative task of blessing and discipling all nations). Over the past two centuries we have understood the breadth of our job really well, but we have neglected its depth.

THE QUANTITATIVE TASK: REACHING EVERY CREATURE

The quantitative task of the church can be measured, mapped, and graphed. We live in perhaps the most exciting time in church history for globally measuring and targeting the unreached.[2] We have amazing amounts of information to help us evaluate our job of spreading the gospel. In the past thirty years whole organizations have been formed solely to track and document how we are doing as a generation of Christians in fulfilling our mandate to reach every person on earth with the gospel.

We know that there are more than six billion people on the planet today. We know that more than 90 percent of those who have never heard the gospel live in what missiologists call the "10/40 Window." This is the area of the world between the northern latitudes of ten and forty degrees, from West Africa across all of Asia. Within this window lies most of the Muslim, Buddhist, Hindu, and Confucian world. We know that fewer than 5 percent of the world's Christian missionaries work inside the 10/40 Window, and the remaining 95 percent or more work where less than 10 percent have never heard the claims of Christ. This gives us a clear picture of where we are to pour our energies if we are going to complete the task of reaching every creature in our generation.

In addition to our awareness of the population and geographic challenges of this task, we know today that some eleven thousand languages in the world still have no witness of Jesus. We know which of these groups have already been targeted by translation ministries and how long it will take them to be reached. Computers, language, and mapping programs have made this an exciting area of research, giving meaningful tools to workers in the field. All of this helps us to evaluate the job the church needs to accomplish and the strategies needed to do it.

We can compare the job of reaching every creature today with the job of the first-generation church. We know that in Paul's day approximately one church existed for every four hundred or more ethnic groups that needed to be reached with the gospel. Today more than four hundred churches exist for each unreached tribe. In the first-generation church there was one Christian for every seven people who had never heard the gospel. Today there are seven Christians for every person who has never heard the gospel. Yes, more people live on the planet today than in all prior human history, but more Christians and more churches are trying to reach them than at any point in human history.

The quantitative task of reaching every creature in this generation is advancing. We can be proud of the church's commitment to this in our age. The work must continue and increase. Our job is to finish, to reach every creature, if God is to be glorified in our generation. But what about teaching, blessing, and discipling all nations? What does this job mean, and are we doing it?

THE QUALITATIVE TASK: DISCIPLING ALL NATIONS

Along with telling the disciples to reach every creature, Jesus reemphasized man's second mandate by telling them to "make disciples of all nations." God's destiny for man, for Israel, for nations, and for the church was never size alone. God is concerned with our quality of life. Discipling individuals and communities is the qualitative work of teaching and applying truth for life-producing growth and maturity.

What does it mean to disciple a nation? What does a discipled nation look like? These are difficult questions, because qualitative evaluations are harder to make. When is a person mature? When is an act great? How do you determine when an economy is developed? What is poor? These questions are even harder in this age, because for the past one to two hundred years we have been focusing almost solely on the quantitative growth of the church. As a result, we have perhaps the largest church in history—and the shallowest.

We may not know what it means to disciple a nation, but surely we know what it does *not* mean. When we look at Dallas, Texas, or Malawi or Rwanda or any other Christianized community or country today, are we willing to say, "This is what it looks like when our job is finished"? Is this God's will done on earth as it is in heaven? Surely not!

If we are to glorify the Father in our generation, we must know what our job is, and do it. We are reaching the unreached, but reached individuals, communities, and nations are living in unacceptable conditions. Dr. George Kinoti, a university professor in Kenya, says,

"The wretchedness of the African people dishonors their Creator. Therefore, every Christian has a moral responsibility to do his or her very best to correct the situation."[3]

It is not enough to reach the unreached. It is not enough to plant churches among those who have no churches. We are to disciple individuals and, through them, disciple their communities and nations. If we do not, we are not fulfilling the purpose for which we were created and given eternal life. Moreover, if we do not disciple the nations, God is not glorified in our generation. He is glorified when we *finish* the work he has left for us to do. Saving souls and planting churches is a beginning. But the quality of those churches and the impact of the lives of the believers on their communities is the litmus test of the quality of our work for Christ. Right now we are failing to do our job well. Christian pollster George Barna finds there is "no significant difference" between the behavior of people in the United States who call themselves born-again Christians and those who do not make that claim. Muslim evangelists in Africa ask, "What does Christianity do for the people?" The answer today is *nothing*. Nothing changes. The churches get bigger. More and more people "get saved." But nothing changes. The people are still poor, diseased, uneducated, and left in political and economic chaos.

We must mourn and weep over this state of affairs in the church today, as Nehemiah did over the condition of Jerusalem.[4] We need to fast and pray because the body of Christ and our communities worldwide are in "great trouble and disgrace." We need to rise up, put on the mind of Christ, and become all he intended the church to be. The question is, how do we do that?

CHAPTER 4

THE CORNFIELD
REVELATION

Now what I am commanding you today is not too difficult for
you or beyond your reach. It is not up in heaven, so that you
have to ask, "Who will ascend into heaven to get it and proclaim
it to us so we may obey it?" Nor is it beyond the sea, so that you
have to ask, "Who will cross the sea to get it and proclaim it to us
so we may obey it?" No, the word is very near you; it is in your
mouth and in your heart so that you may obey it.

DEUTERONOMY 30:11–14

I was somewhere between Boise, Idaho, and Des Moines, Iowa.
I can still picture the wheat and cornfields on both sides of the
car sliding by, mile after mile. The time of day, the angle of the light,
the temperature, the clear blue skies are all as real in my mind at this
moment as they were the day God spoke.

For more than a year it had been clear to me that Christians were
missing a significant part of God's revelation. My generation was
well on its way to reaching every creature with the salvation message
but had no idea what it meant to disciple nations. How could we

regain the wisdom, knowledge, and influence to transform communities with the gospel as the church has done in history? What were the keys? I understood that our gospel message was incomplete, but how would we restore the greater revelation?

In my search I had pursued men and women of God who seemed to see the same deficits in the impact of the church. One man, Tom Marshall, was pastoring a small church in New Zealand. This man of God had an enormous vision of the church's role in building the kingdom of God and its influence on earth. After he spoke at Youth With A Mission's university in Kona, I wept for hours with a broken heart over our diminished gospel. I prayed, "God, you must show us the road back. You must reveal again your great revelations of kingdom life beyond conversion."

Over the next few days I went to Pastor Marshall and asked the same questions I had put to others. I was sure he would have the answer. "Tom, how do we do it? How do we actually disciple the nations? How do we put feet to the vision?" His answer was simple, short, and immediate: "I have no idea! God hasn't revealed that to me." That was all he said. To say that I was crestfallen is truly an understatement. The man with the greatest vision in the area of my search had no answers for me. What hope was there?

That year I was traveling through the grain fields of the Great Plains. I was on a seven-month trip visiting mission bases in America. Driving for a change, instead of flying, was a great relief for me. It gave me wonderful time to process and pray. Before I started the journey, I had asked the Lord to give me a plan for my time in the car. I had been reading through the Bible nearly every year and a half for over twenty years and had read most of the English versions at least once. For my trip I felt God give me the specific goal of *listening* to the entire Bible, from Genesis to Revelation. So I brought along an audio version of the Bible to listen to in the car.

I will never forget that morning in the grain fields. The penny dropped, and everything in my life, from that moment, changed. As I was listening to Deuteronomy, it was as though I was suddenly given ears to *hear* what I had read so many times and never understood. I realized the passage I had just listened to was about law! Moses was teaching civil law. Moses was forming government. Then there was a passage on economics. Then one on the family and health care. Now another on law, and on it went. The light flashed into my poor little brain. Revelation hit like a laser beam. Moses' job was to disciple a nation, to teach a people who had been slaves for four hundred years how to form and run their nation. Moses was to teach Israel God's principles of government, economics, family, priesthood, and every God-given domain of human society. He had forty years in the wilderness to do it, and he had written it all down!

What had I been thinking when I read the books of Moses the first twenty or so times? I had been taught to read the Scriptures looking for certain themes: salvation, sin, forgiveness, prayer, righteousness, and spiritual warfare. I had been reading the books allegorically, even though it is clear that they are historical records of events that took place in time and space. When I read of Israel in bondage to slavery, I saw a message on sin and life without Christ and salvation. When I read about the Jews in the wilderness, I saw the "valley of decision" between the life of sin and God's great promise of salvation. When Israel entered the Promised Land—salvation! They were God's at last. I preached these messages.

These parallels of sin, decision, and salvation are in the Bible, and there is nothing wrong with teaching them. But they are not the primary message of the text. What was happening to Moses was real, not allegorical. He had a real population of Jews, in a real desert, with the real challenge of turning them into a prosperous nation. Moses was discipling a real nation in the truths that would make them great in every area of life, and God inspired him to write it all down for you and me. I knew I would never be able to read the Bible in the same way again. My mind was turned upside down.

MOSES: WHAT A JOB!

What a job Moses had! We think we have needy nations today; look at what he had to deal with! We know that 600,000 able-bodied men left Egypt with Moses.[1] What was the entire population? If we take the number of women and children for each able-bodied man in Jacob's family of seventy when they enter Egypt, it is about 4.5 to 1.[2] At that ratio the number of Israelites leaving Egypt would have been somewhere around 2.7 million. Remember, the Israelites were having problems with the pharaohs because they were multiplying so rapidly that they threatened the balance of the Egyptian population.[3] Furthermore, Israel did not leave Egypt alone. Slaves who were not part of Israel left with them as well. Israel had alien members wandering with them from the very beginning of their wilderness journey. It is no exaggeration to say that Moses was leading more than three million people out of Egypt into the desert.

To put that number in perspective, it amounts to the entire population of New Zealand. The largest refugee situation in modern history was that of the Afghans on the Pakistani border after the invasion by the former Soviet Union. They numbered about two million. Yet, even with the combined resources of the United Nations, the Red Cross, and aid from developed countries, this refugee situation overwhelmed our modern agencies. Moses' people were in far worse circumstances and had no outside help to come to their rescue. The Afghan refugees had a country to go back to. They had homes, schools, businesses, and institutions to which they could return. They had banks, roads, and infrastructures to rebuild even though the Soviet Union had demolished some of them. The Afghans were refugees. But the Jews fleeing Egypt were people without a portfolio. They had no country. They had only a promise.

IMAGINE!

These are a people who have grown from a tribe of seventy to more than three million in 430 years.[4] They have been in exile this entire time. For the last 400 years they have been doing slave labor under Egyptian pharaohs. They have just walked out of the nation of Egypt with what they are able to carry and with the animals they own. Think about it! A US Army Quartermaster General put his mathematical mind to the situation and figured they would require approximately 1,500 tons of food per day (two freight trains' worth, each two miles long), 4,000 tons of firewood to cook the food each day, plus one million gallons of water daily to drink and wash the dishes. Their campgrounds would have been two-thirds the size of Rhode Island State. Plus:

- They are poor.
- They have no schools.
- They have no government.
- They have no economy.
- They have no land.
- They have no army.
- They have no industry.
- They have no agriculture.
- They have no religious system.
- They have a welfare mentality and no work ethic.
- They have been oppressed and victimized.
- They have an undeveloped social system.

They are, without a doubt, the largest, most undeveloped mass of people that has ever existed on the face of the earth. Compared to any nation I can think of today, Israel was in much worse shape.

It is to these people that God says, "You are not a people, but I will make you a people." He promises these people, in their poor condition, that they will become a great nation and that other nations will admire their greatness and be blessed by them.[5] The Jews have just left one of the greatest civilizations in human history, Egypt, in its glory day under the pharaohs. They are an impoverished mob in the middle of a wasteland. Yet God says he will make them a great nation! Can you imagine the unbelief, the bewilderment, even the cynicism they might have felt?

In about three hundred years' time, however, God does it. He makes them one of the greatest, if not the greatest nation on the face of the earth. They have such a reputation that within three centuries the whole known world is talking about Israel. A queen from the Arabian peninsula hears of this great kingdom and wants to see it firsthand. She travels north, bypassing Egypt, the former greatest nation. Her journey continues farther north toward Canaan.

1 Kings 10:1–10

When the queen of Sheba heard about the fame of Solomon and his relation to the name of the LORD, she came to test him with hard questions. Arriving at Jerusalem with a very great caravan— with camels carrying spices, large quantities of gold, and precious stones—she came to Solomon and talked with him about all that she had on her mind. Solomon answered all her questions; nothing was too hard for the king to explain to her. When the queen of Sheba saw all the wisdom of Solomon and the palace he had built, the food on his table, the seating of his officials, the attending servants in their robes, his cupbearers, and the burnt offerings he made at the temple of the LORD, she was overwhelmed.

She said to the king, "The report I heard in my own country about your achievements and your wisdom is true. But I did not believe these things until I came and saw with my own eyes. Indeed, not even half was told me; in wisdom and wealth you have far exceeded the report I heard. How happy your men must be! How happy your officials, who continually stand before you and hear your wisdom! Praise be to the LORD your God, who has delighted in you and placed you on the throne of Israel. Because of the LORD's eternal love for Israel, he has made you king, to maintain justice and righteousness."

And she gave the king 120 talents of gold, large quantities of spices, and precious stones. Never again were so many spices brought in as those the queen of Sheba gave to King Solomon.

A PROMISE FULFILLED

God had made a promise to build a great nation, and he did it. He built a great nation in every category. Israel had just laws. They were economically prosperous. Their architecture and crafts were brilliant. They had superior education and wisdom. One of their kings, Solomon, was a great scientist. They were even admired by their former slave masters, the Egyptians. They were by no means a perfect kingdom; God had never indicated that he was promising that. But they were a great kingdom. This history of Israel is not written as an allegory from which we are to learn the spiritual benefits of salvation, although you could make that point from the text. This is history—it happened in time and space to real people, to a real nation. The point for us is: if God did it once, he can do it again.

God's truth, if applied, can and does transform communities and nations. If God can develop these impoverished Jews into a great nation, he can do it for any existing nation in any age, because not one community or nation in the world today is worse off than the Israelites in that wilderness. God has told us to reach every creature with the message of salvation, and he has taught us how to do that. He left us the models of Jesus and Paul and the New Testament church to guide us into the global vision of reaching every language, every tribe, and every people. But God has also told us to disciple every nation. How do we do that? God has not given us a job and then been silent on how to accomplish it. Just as the keys to evangelism are in the stories of Jesus and Paul, the keys to our job in transforming communities are in the story of Moses. Israel—its journey from slavery to greatness—is our Old Testament template of how to disciple a nation.

Now the question is, will we learn how to use it? Will we take the time to study God's Word until our minds have been restored, until we understand God's principles of community building and nation building in every arena of life? Will we do the work of being reformed in our generation so that God can once again glorify himself through the wisdom and influence of his people? We must decide. You must decide.

CHAPTER 5

LEARNING TO COLOR...
AGAIN!

Then all the people went away to eat and drink, to send portions
of food and to celebrate with great joy, because they now understood the words that had been made known to them.
NEHEMIAH 8:12

He sent forth his word and healed them; he rescued them from
the grave.
PSALM 107:20

As the woman boarded the plane and walked through my section, she peered into my open briefcase and asked, "Will we be
coloring on the flight today?" There in my bag beside my Bible lay
eight colored pencils. As soon as I had realized what God was saying to me in the grain fields, I knew what I must do. At first chance
I would buy colored pencils and a new Bible to study what God's
Word teaches about each area of influence in society—government,
economics, family, and so forth. I would start with the books of
Moses, because it was Moses' job to teach a nation these things. Then

I would work my way through the rest of the Bible to see the whole counsel of God's Word on any given domain. I don't think I had been this excited about something since the invention of television.

I already had an idea of the domains I would study in Scripture because the University of the Nations, where I was Founding International Dean of the College of Communication, had been developed around the concept of the spheres of influence in society. I chose government, economics, family, science (including technology), arts and entertainment, communication, education, and the traditional work of the church. My thought, as I began, was that the very study itself would confirm whether or not these were primary categories in God's Word. The nature of the search was to discover how much each category was emphasized and what principles were given. At this same time, I came across a Bible color-coded by the traditional salvation and witnessing themes. It's a wonderful tool for studying what the Bible has to say about those subjects, and I was encouraged that I was on the right track in using different colors for studying each domain. I started coloring.

THE BIBLE STUDY HEADACHE

From day one, this study was so intense that I could do only twenty or thirty minutes at a time. It required such a radical shift from how I'd been trained to read the Word that it gave me a headache. I felt my eyes were being distorted in their sockets. I was so profoundly affected in the reading that I would have to get up, pace the room, and pray for help to absorb all that God was saying, all that I had missed in nearly thirty years of Bible study. My secular/sacred, dichotomized mind kept rising up in rebellion against what I saw in the Word, accusing me of socializing the gospel and secularizing the Word of God. But as I prayed and studied and sought God's help, I saw that God was teaching about all of life. God was teaching government. If this was secular, then God was secular. It was not my place to tell God in what arenas he could involve himself. It was, rather, God's place to tell *me* what his kingdom comprised.

Day after day for five years, my mind was blown by the lost gospel of the kingdom. I saw, time and again, where great men and women of God found the principles they had used to change and disciple their nations—principles and values that are clear in Scripture, values to which we still give lip service in so-called Christian nations, principles we no longer teach, no longer understand, and can no longer articulate with the authority of Scripture behind them.

I grieved to see how much of the Word of God we no longer use because it does not fit what we emphasize and teach. I realized how much Scripture we distort beyond recognition in order to teach our own interests. This process of relearning the Bible was deeply personal. I had spent my life studying and teaching these very distortions. I had traveled to nearly half the world's nations, giving them less than 20 percent of God's counsel. For more than half of my life I had led discipleship programs that never touched on 80 percent of the nature and character of God and his perfect ways in all of life.

UNSURPASSABLE GREATNESS

While I grieved that I had seen only a small portion of God's revelation, I also rejoiced and worshiped the God who was being revealed to me. I wanted to run from my study and shout from the rooftops, "You have no idea how great God is! You have no idea how great God's good news is!" My heart raced with the revelation of the completeness and unsurpassable greatness of the lordship of Christ and his kingdom. Salvation, and the life that it gave me, was the turning point in my life, but it was nothing compared to this daily revelation of the rest of the gospel and the greatness of God's kingdom.

In reducing the gospel to salvation alone, we had also reduced our revelation of God to Savior alone. Indeed, he is our Savior. This is a wonderful revelation, essential to entering the gates of his kingdom. However, we have lost the revelation of the King of Kings, the Lord of justice; of Jehovah Jireh, Lord of economics; of the Father, Lord of the family; of the creator God, Lord of science and technology; of the living Word, Lord of communication; of the Potter, Lord of the arts and beauty; and of the great Teacher, Lord of education. We use these names and worship with these images, but we no longer understand the supremacy of Christ in each of these domains and vocations.

WE HAVE A MINIATURE JESUS

Today we reflect a "miniature" Jesus by getting saved and then standing inside the door of the kingdom, calling others to salvation. We do not know how to move past the cloakroom into the greatness of God in all of life. We don't know how to think about God's political agenda. We don't know what the gospel has to say about building our lives and communities economically. We don't know how to keep our marriages together. We don't have time for "secular" activities like the arts. We huddle in the foyer of God's great mansion and try to define ourselves there because our lives have less and less to do with the outside world. Is it any wonder, then, that we fixate on experiences and feelings, seeking refuge from the world we live in rather than engaging it? If our minds are not challenged and we are closed off from all of life, what is left?

For nearly a decade at this writing, I have been looking at the Scriptures from the perspective of God's teaching on the domains. I have colored my entire Bible many times with what God says about government, education, economics, family, the arts, communication, science, and the church. Daily my mind, my spirit, and my heart explode with gratitude for who God is and the treasures he has given us in Christ Jesus. I am not ashamed of this gospel, because it is relevant to all of humanity's needs and all the issues we face today.

In Part II, I begin describing this more complete understanding of the nature and character of God as revealed in all that he has made. These ideas just scratch the surface of the Word. This is a lifetime study, and I am calling you to join me on the journey, the journey back to the gospel of the kingdom—the journey back to the God of all things.

PART II

How Do We
Get Started?

INTRODUCTION

In Part II we begin to look at what the Bible teaches us about the various domains of society and the principles that are to guide us in our involvement in these arenas. It is important to remember that this volume of The Old Testament Template is an introduction to the concepts and ideas. It is in no way exhaustive of what the Bible has to say about each domain. In future works I hope to look at each domain more completely from all of Scripture. But that research is still in process. Here we are trying to learn how to study and rethink what Scripture has to say about these areas. In reordering our thinking to match the mind of Christ, it is important for us to do so carefully and methodically, establishing precepts, digesting them, incorporating them into our lives in obedience to truth and Christ's lordship, and *then* ask the Holy Spirit to lead us to the next level of understanding. I am trying to follow this radical obedience in my own life and mind, resisting the temptation to run off with a lot of easy and premature conclusions. People ask me every time I teach to draw conclusions and applications to current events that I am simply not prepared to make yet. God is renewing my mind. God is taking my thinking captive. It is a process, and the most destructive thing we can do is to get ahead of him, thinking we know more about the Word of God than we actually do. Lord, help us in our temptations.

In this section we will look at examples of what the Bible, primarily the book of Deuteronomy, teaches us about each domain and how to track those principles through the rest of Scripture. There are many principles on many levels in every domain. We will only look at a few. The main point is to begin changing how we read and think about Scripture in ways that move us toward an integrated view of God and all of life. We have used Deuteronomy as the basis of most of the introduction because the Jewish scholars accepted it as the foundational book of what Moses taught in all his writings. All future scholarship, including that of Jesus and Paul, references Moses and the teachings imparted by God through him as the foundation stones of biblical thinking.

Each domain reveals attributes of God's character and nature. Each domain reveals truths about his kingdom and how it functions. When we study these areas, we are learning about God—not only what he does but who he is! It is essential that we keep this as our focus and our passion. If we study with strategy and action as our focus, we will miss the heart of the message. God's primary objective is not to get us to fulfill a job for him, even one as important as reaching and discipling the nations. God's desire is to reveal himself to us. He wants us to know him! This humbles my heart. This humbles my mind. What kind of God is this that cares so much for you and me that he desires to know and to be known with such intimacy?

This truth of God's priorities must supersede all other motives in our search for a relevant gospel to the issues of the twenty-first century. It is not, first and foremost, about us and what we are to do. It is about him!

Chapter 6

Government

And the government will be on his shoulders.
Isaiah 9:6

This is also why you pay taxes, for the authorities are God's servants, who give their full time to governing.
Romans 13:6

For more than a generation many, if not most, Christians have thought of the domain of government as the bastion of cigar-smoking egomaniacs. I have heard prominent Christians say that they see no way a Christian could be involved in politics without compromising his or her faith in Christ. This thinking is so extreme in parts of the body of Christ that some churches teach their members not to vote. This is a profound example of the split thinking of "secular" versus "sacred."

When the blacks in Namibia were first given the vote in 1994, they elected a government perceived to be communist, a heavy blow in a country where more than 85 percent of the population were professing Christians. But there was a ray of hope when the newly seated government sent word to church leaders in the nation that they wanted representatives of the church to come and teach them the biblical basis of government. What a privilege! But no one responded! In South Africa, the ruling party today (holding 65 percent of the vote, of which around 70 percent is Christian) struggles to stay in power, in part, they say, because the theology of some churches has produced a nonparticipatory culture among Christians when it comes to social, political, and economic issues. I am told by American government officials that far less than 50 percent of American citizens vote. Even more shocking, they say that less than 25 percent of American Christians vote.

All of this is a far cry from the respect Paul accorded those who served in the government arena.[1] Jesus understood that government had a role in his Father's kingdom. He was discipled *by* the Old Testament, and he discipled *with* the Old Testament. Jesus, the King of Kings, understood that his message was a message of salvation and a message of political justice.

THE KING OF KINGS

When we study the domain of government in the Bible, we are looking at the legislative, executive, judicial, and military functions of government. We are looking at law, national and local authority, relationships between nations, rules of war, and areas of community development related to government. We are looking at the roles and actions of judges and kings and those who worked for them in official capacities. Books like Joshua, Judges, 1 and 2 Samuel, 1 and 2 Kings, and 1 and 2 Chronicles unfold events happening in and to Israel in the political arena. They document what the political leaders of Israel were doing, how they affected Israel, and what God thought about these events. Nehemiah, Esther, and Daniel tell us the stories of people who sought to serve God faithfully in the political arena. Interestingly, Nehemiah, Esther, and Daniel each served in pagan and idolatrous nations and kingdoms. Today some Christians believe we should serve in government only under righteous leaders, but Scripture does not bear this out. In addition, Psalms, Proverbs, Ecclesiastes, and Song of Solomon were written primarily by two kings, David and Solomon. Each of these books teaches us much besides the principles of government, but they were written from the perspective of government, unlike Isaiah, Jeremiah, and other books written from the perspective of prophets.

In my study of Deuteronomy, I discovered that about 25 percent of the book pertains to instructions and episodes revolving around government issues. The passage we will use for our sample study of the domain of government is Deuteronomy 1:9–18. Moses had been attempting to sit as judge by himself over the disputes of the entire Israelite population. His father-in-law had suggested to him that this was not going to work and that he needed to initiate levels of government to carry the load of arbitrating the judicial needs of the nation. In Deuteronomy Moses forms Israel's first system of government. Here is the account:

Deuteronomy 1:9–18

At that time I said to you, "You are too heavy a burden for me to carry alone. The LORD *your God has increased your numbers so that today you are as many as the stars in the sky. May the* LORD, *the God of your fathers, increase you a thousand times and bless you as he has promised! But how can I bear your problems and your burdens and your disputes all by myself? Choose some wise, understanding and respected men from each of your tribes, and I will set them over you."*

You answered me, "What you propose to do is good."

So I took the leading men of your tribes, wise and respected men, appointed them to have authority over you—as commanders of thousands, of hundreds, of fifties and of tens and as tribal officials. And I charged your judges at that time: Hear the disputes between your brothers and judge fairly, whether the case is between brother Israelites or between one of them and an alien. Do not show partiality in judging; hear both small and great alike.

*Do not be afraid of any man, for judgment belongs to God. Bring
me any case too hard for you, and I will hear it. And at that time I
told you everything you were to do.*

For our purpose here of learning to read and study the Bible
in order to see God's principles in each domain, we will take only
the highlights of the passage. Remember that the truths of the Bible
are told primarily in story form. We study the history and context,
but we will never be in the same circumstances as Moses and Israel,
so their application will not necessarily work for us. The principles,
however, are God's truth and are applicable in new and dynamic
ways in any age, any set of circumstances in any nation. Let's work
with this passage as an example of extracting principles from the
historical situation.

THE PURPOSE OF GOVERNMENT

Deuteronomy 1:9–12
*At that time I said to you, "You are too heavy a burden for me to
carry alone. The LORD your God has increased your numbers so
that today you are as many as the stars in the sky. May the LORD,
the God of your fathers, increase you a thousand times and bless
you as he has promised! But how can I bear your problems and
your burdens and your disputes all by myself?*

As Moses prepared to form Israel's first formal government, he
explained to the people the purpose of government and why Israel
needed to move away from him as their sole leader. Moses had been
carrying the load by himself until now. But this system no longer
fulfilled the objective of government. What was that objective?
Moses saw it as his responsibility to hear the burdens and disputes of
the people in order to provide just resolution. He did not see disputes
as insignificant matters or a waste of time, nor did he argue that the
people ought not to be disputing in the first place. He established
that disputes must be heard and dealt with, but Israel had grown so

large in Egypt that the former tribal system of governing themselves no longer worked. They needed a more effective system. Why? To meet the judicial needs of the people.

One of the foundational principles in this passage is that the primary purpose of government is to serve the population of a nation by providing an objective, trustworthy source of arbitration and justice. The system of government was organized in such a way that it could serve the needs of people, "both small and great alike" (v. 17). God looked at the judicial needs of the people and saw that the current system was not meeting those needs. He inspired Moses to create a structure of government that would meet the judicial needs of the nation, and Moses set out to put it in place.

THE AUTHORITY OF GOVERNMENT

Deuteronomy 1:13
"Choose some wise, understanding and respected men from each of your tribes, and I will set them over you."

From the perspective of government, I think this is one of the most thrilling verses in the Bible. Think about it. This group of people had lived in exile for 430 years. For 400 of those years they had been slaves under the authority of the Egyptian government. Their experience of leadership prior to their years in Egypt was more that of a large family, some seventy people. We can assume that many of the Jews, if not most, were uneducated. They had lived in poverty, and the Egyptians had no reason to expend their national budget to educate their slaves. When the Jews fled Egypt, they were in the wilderness, exiles in no man's land, with no assets except what they carried on their backs.

Moses was God's man, a man who spoke with God face to face. God had been giving Moses detailed instructions for leading Israel to freedom. He had given Moses incredible authority by bringing to pass everything Moses said would happen. If anyone ever had a direct line to God, it was Moses. When he formed government in

Israel, how did God tell him to do it? He told Moses to say, "Choose some wise, understanding and respected men. . . ." Who chose the leadership? Moses? Aaron and Miriam? No, the people of Israel! The very first thing that God did through Moses when establishing government was to give the people the right and authority to choose.

What an amazing God! In all of his infinite knowledge and wisdom God did not impose his will. He could have said to Moses, "You choose some wise and understanding men and put them over Israel." That would have been more like the model they had seen in Egypt. That would have been more like what was being modeled by the tribal nations surrounding them. But God did something so radical, so dangerous, so not of this world, that we are still trying to grapple with the principle in our modern age. He gave the people of Israel the right to choose their political leaders.

We could say, then, that a second principle of government is that God gives the authority of governance to the people. God delegated to the people, by law and decree, the right and responsibility of choosing who would rule over them. He made it a bottom-up authority as opposed to the top-down authority of the Egyptian pharaohs. He gave the people power.

Many people today, in and out of Christian circles, believe the important thing is to tell the public what to do. We often assume that people do not have the experience, the education, the grasp of issues to make proper choices. Surely it would be better to start them off gradually and nurture them into the process of responsibility. But God began the process of discipling Israel in their new freedom by giving them the responsibility to choose who would lead them.

This principle is supported throughout the biblical history of Israel. They were a nation ruled by judges for some 470 years. They observed and interacted with the nations surrounding them and saw that these nations had kings. Israel began to like this idea. They had some good judges, but they had some real losers, topped off by the notorious Samson. They decided they needed a king, and told this to Samuel, the prophet to the nation.[2] Samuel sought God, and God responded very clearly. He did *not* want them to have a king, and he gave them a very sizable list of reasons why. But the people persisted. They wanted a king! God relented and told Samuel they could choose what they wanted.

Think about this. God gave them the king that he did not want because that is what they chose. A king was not the best choice, but this is what they as a nation chose. God had given the people the authority to choose their political leaders, and having made his preference known, he stuck to that principle. Once Israel determined to have a king, God helped them choose one. God went beyond sticking to his principles; he sought to bless the kings that Israel chose. Saul, David, Solomon, and other kings were mightily used by God, but a monarchy was still not the system of governance that God wanted for his people.

Perhaps you are thinking, "But didn't the prophets actually choose the kings?" This is fascinating to track in Scripture. God did use the prophets to point to the leader who would serve the nation's best interests. At God's direction they anointed these leaders with oil and prayed and prophesied over them.[3] But we do not see a king in Israel actually crowned king until we hear words like, "All Israel gathered and took so-and-so as their king."[4] After the people made their choice, the king realized his authority.

This principle of the authority of the people to choose their political leaders is tested in the life of David. When Saul died, the kingdom of Israel was divided over who would lead them. The house of Judah had chosen Saul's rival, David, who had already been anointed to be king over Israel by Samuel. But Saul had a son, Ish-Bosheth, and Israel chose him to be their king. Two leaders of Ish-Bosheth's raiding bands decided David should be king of Israel as well as Judah. They murdered Ish-Bosheth and took his head to David. Rather than accept their offer to be king, David executed them for the murder.[5] He remained in Hebron until all the tribes of Israel came to David and asked him to be king.[6] David understood, having studied the books of Moses, that God had given the authority of choosing political leaders to the people.

Why would God design government to have its authority in the people? Wouldn't it be better for people to be told by a loving, benevolent God what is best for them? Evidently not. This subject is too broad to cover in this introductory volume, but it appears that the discipleship of a nation, as well as individuals, is tied to the cause-and-effect learning process of experiencing the blessing or curse that results from making choices. In other words, it was more important for Israel to make their choice, even if it was not a perfect choice, and to learn from the consequences. Weighty implications, but they will have to wait for future study.

CHARACTER DOES MATTER

Deuteronomy 1:13
"Choose some wise, understanding and respected men . . ."

God did not leave Israel floundering in a vacuum with their choices of political leaders. He gave them guidelines. Some of those guidelines focused on character, knowledge, and the leader's reputation. A Nigerian friend once said to me that one of the big differences between a Westerner and an African is the standard they use to judge the importance of an individual. A Westerner, he felt, was more prone to assess a person by what he owned, what he did, or his position. An African, on the other hand, drew his or her assessment of an individual from what other people thought about that person. In other words, you had status in the tribe if the community gave you status, not because of some external, such as possessions or your work. The African approach is more relational and is tied to the character and observable actions of the individual within a community setting. If my friend is correct, then God, it would appear, leans toward the African perspective when it comes to political leaders. The people were made responsible to assess the character of the leaders they would grant political power and then live with the consequences of their choices.

Moses gave Israel three things to look for in their leaders—wisdom, understanding, and respectability. Money and power, though not disqualified, are not mentioned as criteria. In order for these character attributes to be evaluated, the leaders had to be known by the people and the people had to determine what "wise, understanding, and respected" meant. What made an individual respectable? How was wisdom demonstrated? What did it mean to have understanding? As a community they not only had to search for an individual who embodied these qualities, but they had to search for understanding about the nature of those qualities. They would enter a national debate on character, if you will. God was developing them as citizens, not just giving them government.

REPRESENTATIVE

Deuteronomy 1:13
". . . from each of your tribes . . ."

From the time Israel left Egypt, God began to emphasize the importance of inclusion in the political and legal process. He reminded Israel that they must remember what it was like to be slaves who had no rights. He reminded them repeatedly that they were not to have one standard of justice for the Israelite and another for the alien. They were not to leave any tribe without representation in their new land and government. Political representation is a biblical principle. If the purpose of government is to arbitrate disputes and issues of justice, and if the authority of government comes from the people, then the people have to be represented.

The great error of the South African government of the twentieth century was that one white tribe declared the right to rule over all other tribes. The right to vote was extended only to the white tribes. The black tribes were left without representation. If we understand these scriptures and recognize that God could not bless a system that left a people disenfranchised from the powers that ruled over them, then it comes as no surprise that the South African government of this era could achieve no lasting stability. In principle it was doomed to fail. But understanding here will also lead to great admiration for the leadership of Nelson Mandela and his commitment not to form a government unless every black tribe and every white tribe was represented. The upholding of this principle safeguarded the nation and held civil war at bay. When we think of the Aboriginals in Australia, the Sami in Finland, and the Native Americans, we are seeing situations fraught with potential conflict because the principle of representation has been diluted or ignored altogether.

CONSENSUS

Deuteronomy 1:14
You answered me, "What you propose to do is good."

The authority of the people is reinforced again. In this very short sentence Moses established that his plan had the backing of the nation. Israel agreed to be governed in this way.

Israel had not always agreed with Moses. In his first attempt to take them into the Promised Land, they said in fear and unbelief that they would not go. They staged what we would call today a military coup, and the men of fighting age refused to take on the challenge of entering the Promised Land in spite of Moses', Joshua's, and Caleb's exhortations.[7] God was ready for them to move into the Promised Land. Moses was ready for them to move. The people were not in agreement. The government lacked consensus and could not move ahead. Israel suffered the consequences of their choices by spending forty years in the wilderness. In the account of David's appointment as king over Israel, the house of Judah and the house of Saul did not have consensus; David waited rather than contesting the will of the people.[8]

This principle of consensus is so important that Jesus refers to it as a principle of God's kingdom in the New Testament. "Every kingdom divided against itself will be ruined."[9] The principle is this: a nation with consensus has a more stable government. A nation without consensus is a weakened nation. Therefore a government that tries to impose its will on the people will be less stable in the long term than a government that rules with consensus. Consensus is one of the foundations of strong government.

This gives us understanding when we look at nations in crisis and at specific national issues. Ireland, like South Africa, has been on the front pages of world news for a long time because of its great turmoil. In *How the Irish Saved Civilization* Thomas Cahill reveals that the Irish have never been able to agree on who governed them. For the eight-thousand-plus years of Irish history, their kings and tribes have been at war. The failure of a few attempts to rule themselves with an Irish king led them to seek French, Scottish, and finally English monarchs to rule over them. The failure to find any semblance of consensus has led to millennia of turmoil. Conversely, it makes the importance of the Irish accord signed in the 1990s even more resounding. For perhaps the first time in their very long history, the Irish are beginning to see that agreement and consensus are essential if the nation is to rule itself. God is discipling Ireland.

When we look at situations today such as East Timor, former Yugoslavia, and the former Soviet Union, we are seeing, in part, the consequences of rule forced on people with little or no involvement, let alone any level of consensus.

THE JUDICIAL BRANCH

Deuteronomy 1:16–18

And I charged your judges at that time: Hear the disputes between your brothers and judge fairly, whether the case is between brother Israelites or between one of them and an alien. Do not show partiality in judging; hear both small and great alike. Do not be afraid of any man, for judgment belongs to God. Bring me any case too hard for you, and I will hear it. And at that time I told you everything you were to do.

Now Moses turned his attention to the judicial purpose of government and began to give instructions to those who would hear the disputes of the people. These verses lay down such powerful principles of justice that every just court in the world uses them, and every court on earth today would be more just if the principles were thoroughly implemented. First, verse 16 exhorts Israel's judges to judge fairly. Moses goes on to define *fairly* very specifically. *Fairly* means extending the same quality of justice to every individual whether they are Israelite or alien, national or foreigner. This is a major theme in God's discipleship of Israel. Over and over again in their biblical history, God reminds them of what it was like to be slaves under the authority of Egypt, what it was like to be foreigners unjustly treated, and what it was like to be disenfranchised from the justice system of the nation they lived in. He used this tragic part of their history to call them to a higher level of justice in their own nation. Justice in Israel was to be blind to nationality, color, gender, creed, or politics. Justice was to have a level playing field and to treat all people equally.

In verse 17 Moses exhorts Israel's judicial system to *judge without partiality*, further stating that their court system was not to draw a distinction between "small and great." Justice in Israel was not to be tilted toward the powerful and influential or the rich. All people were to be heard. The slave in Egypt had no voice, and God told Israel that they were to demonstrate a higher level of justice in their nation.

Moses reminded them that justice belongs to God. As judges, they were not to be afraid of other people, powers, or influences. They were to remember that as governmental agents of justice they stood first and foremost before God. God understood that the human race was fallen and prone to sin and that the Jews, being human, would be just as prone to corruption as any other group of people or any nation. He was challenging them to rise above this in their system of government.

Moses laid down the last principle of the judicial system in this passage. There is to be a process of appeal. For cases too hard for a finding, or when findings and evidence were inconclusive, the system allowed another hearing—this time before Moses.

Some years ago I was privileged to speak at a conference where a head of state sat directly before me in the front row. This Christian man was the president of a pagan nation. His desire was to use his office to influence his nation for righteousness. When I inquired about the judicial system in his country, I found that the president hires and fires at will all judges in this nation. In this system a judge faced with a less than obvious finding, knowing he could lose his livelihood, might favor the preference of the president who holds his job in his hand. The president could move his nation toward God by changing the justice system so that the position of a judge is secure from the whims of political leaders. Nevertheless, God never forgets that humanity is fallen, and he lays down every principle and system with our fallen state in mind. One judge can be corrupted some of the time, but it is harder to corrupt two judges in an appeal, and so forth. God understands that without checks and balances in the system, fallen people will abuse power and corrupt justice.

SUMMARY

We looked at five basic principles of government from ten verses in Deuteronomy.

1. Government is ordained by God and essential to the life of a nation.
2. Government gets its authority from the people.
3. The character of a political leader is important and to be weighed by the people in their choices.
4. Government is to be representative of all people.
5. One of government's primary purposes is to provide a source of just resolution to disputes and conflicts of the people.

The intent of this introductory volume is not to teach a complete biblical approach to government or any other domain. Our purpose is to reveal how our split Christian thinking has alienated us from God's great wisdom and teaching in each domain and to demonstrate how God's Word teaches us principles for all of life, as we have seen in these verses on government. To have the mind of Christ on government, we must study the subject from Genesis to

Revelation, discerning the whole counsel of God. This will take time and patience. It took Moses forty years to lay down God's teaching in the wilderness. We need a generation of faithful Bible students to help us reinherit the truth.

As someone has said, peace is not just the absence of conflict; it is the presence of justice. When we pray for peace, let us remember that God calls us to work for justice.

STUDY HELP

- Themes to look for in studying and coloring government in the Scriptures: *law; government; the military; legislative, executive, and judicial branches of government; national and local authority; and community development from the legislative or executive perspective*
- The domain of government reveals: *the King of Kings*
- The primary attribute of God revealed in government: *justice*
- God governs this domain through: *delegation of authority to the people*
- The color I used: *purple*

WORKING VOCATIONAL MISSION STATEMENT

To provide and ensure justice and equity for all citizens through executive, judicial, military, law enforcement, and central community services (e.g., water, power, roads, education).

Great issues include justice for the weak and voiceless in society, including children, women, and immigrants.

A NOTE TO ALL BELIEVERS

God is calling you to be a good citizen as part of the witness of your faith. Political action and interest are not "secular" in the sense that they are not important for believers. God instituted government, and he gave you and me responsibility for it. God is just and wants all his people to work for justice. First of all, it is our responsibility under God to be informed and to be involved. Do you vote? If you live in a country where participation is allowed, it is your moral obligation as a Christian to be involved. If you live in a country where you are denied that right, you must pray and work to see your nation's legal system changed. As believers we should be volunteering at the polls, helping people get registered, and making it possible to have a place to vote.

We should explain to our children that God gave us this great right and responsibility to be involved in our political life, and we must cherish and safeguard this right. We are to teach our children that serving in government is a high calling and that if God has gifted them in this area, he may call them and favor them as he did David, Daniel, Joseph, Nehemiah, and others. If this is the case, they will have a much higher purpose in their occupations than "just making money"; they will be serving God. They must have the mind of Christ, the power of the Holy Spirit, and strategic prayer support if their work is to accomplish something of lasting value for the kingdom.

You are God's strategy for discipling your community and nation. Will you respond to the call?

A NOTE TO THE GOVERNMENT PROFESSIONAL

If you are a lawyer, judge, police officer, civil servant, soldier, elected official, or social worker or you serve your nation's government in any other capacity, you have a high calling from God. The pillars of God's kingdom are justice and righteousness, and your calling is to support the pillar of justice. You are challenged by Scripture to be God's extension of justice to the people you serve. It does not matter whether you work in a system that is fair, as Solomon did, or in one that is somewhat or thoroughly unjust, as Joseph and Daniel did. You have a calling from God to give and work for the highest level of justice possible in the system. First, you must be just in your own dealings with people. Then you must work to make the institutions, systems, and laws just. What would your nation look like if every Christian professional made this his or her passion and pursued it with a sense of call? God will start with one. Are you that one? Will you study to take on the mind of Christ in the political arena and apply what you are learning first to your own life and work and then where possible to the institutions themselves? You are God's strategy for discipling your nation.

CHAPTER 7

ECONOMICS

However, there should be no poor among you, for in the land the
LORD your God is giving you to possess as your inheritance, he
will richly bless you.
DEUTERONOMY 15:4

For the kingdom of heaven is like a landowner who went out
early in the morning to hire men to work in his vineyard.
MATTHEW 20:1

*M*oney is the root of all evil! Filthy lucre! Common enough
ideas in the minds of many Christians today. "If you love
God, you will despise material gain" is a prevalent undercurrent in
Christianity. "If I truly love God, I will probably be poor" is perhaps
not taught, but it is surely thought. The split thinking that creates a
false divide between the spiritual and material is as glaringly obvious
in this domain as any other. God's promises to Israel as they left slavery in Egypt were not confined to blessings of an unseen nature. He
promised he would bless them in every area of life, including their

crops, livestock, and businesses. He encouraged that if they would obey his teachings, they would not have poverty in their land. God fulfilled his promise. In little more than three hundred years Israel moved from living in abject poverty in the wilderness to being one of the wealthiest nations in its day.

It is also not uncommon today to find believers who think of money more in terms of magic than in terms of biblical principles. "If I give this amount, I will get this amount back! God will drop provision from the sky. I am believing for a miracle in my finances." Please understand me here! I am not against tithing. I believe God can and does perform financial miracles, and I believe God honors and blesses the generous heart. However, this thinking, when separated from Scripture's overarching principles of finance, is not biblical thinking; it is mysticism.

For most of the first two millennia of church growth, economic change and development followed the spread of the gospel. Moses taught that Israel was to have no poor, and the early church began to deal with poverty in its earliest agendas. Moses taught that work was part of our service to God, and Paul reaffirmed this in the New Testament by teaching that believers who did not work did not eat.[1] In Norway the evangelist Hans Nielsen Hauge (1771–1824) worked his way from one desperately poor village to another. As he planted churches, he also taught biblical business practices and helped new converts start businesses. Not only did the gospel win souls in Scandinavia and the rest of western Europe, but it fed an economic revolution.

This is a far cry from the fruit the gospel has produced over the last two centuries. Africa provides us with our most stark reality. In his book *Hope for Africa and What the Christian Can Do,* Dr. George Kinoti lays out the following crucial observations: One out of every three Africans does not get enough to eat. By 1987, 55 to 60 percent of rural Africans were living below the poverty line, and the rate of impoverishment is accelerating. Two-thirds of the poorest forty nations in the world are African, as are eight of the poorest ten nations. "Experts tell us that Christianity is growing faster in Africa than on any other continent. At the same time, the people are rapidly becoming poorer and the moral and social fabric of society are disintegrating fast. Christianity is clearly not making a significant difference to African nations."[2]

Let's look at a key economic passage from Moses' teaching in Deuteronomy:

Deuteronomy 15:1–10

At the end of every seven years you must cancel debts. This is how it is to be done: Every creditor shall cancel the loan he has made to his fellow Israelite. He shall not require payment from his fellow Israelite or brother, because the LORD's time for canceling debts has been proclaimed. You may require payment from a foreigner, but you must cancel any debt your brother owes you. However, there should be no poor among you, for in the land the LORD your God is giving you to possess as your inheritance, he will richly bless you, if only you fully obey the LORD your God and are careful to follow all these commands I am giving you today. For the LORD your God will bless you as he has promised, and you will lend to many nations but will borrow from none. You will rule over many nations but none will rule over you.

If there is a poor man among your brothers in any of the towns of the land that the LORD your God is giving you, do not be hardhearted or tightfisted toward your poor brother. Rather be openhanded and freely lend him whatever he needs. Be careful not to harbor this wicked thought: "The seventh year, the year for canceling debts, is near," so that you do not show ill will toward your needy brother and give him nothing. He may then appeal to the LORD against you, and you will be found guilty of sin. Give generously to him and do so without a grudging heart; then because of this the LORD your God will bless you in all your work and in everything you put your hand to.

God makes it clear throughout Scripture that he desires to bless *all* nations.[3] When we ask, "How does God want to bless them?" we find the answer in how he blessed Israel. Economic blessing was a clear part of God's design for Israel from the moment they left Egypt. In Deuteronomy 15 we see that while they are still in the wilderness, he is preparing them for economic development and their responsibility to both the individual and the nation.

DEBT IS TO BE LIMITED

Deuteronomy 15:1–3

At the end of every seven years you must cancel debts. This is how it is to be done: Every creditor shall cancel the loan he has made to his fellow Israelite. He shall not require payment from his fellow Israelite or brother, because the LORD's time for canceling debts has been proclaimed. You may require payment from a foreigner, but you must cancel any debt your brother owes you.

When I speak in various countries, I often ask how many in my audience have heard the teaching that Christians should never borrow. No matter what region of the world I am in, a few have been exposed to this message. The text often used for this teaching is Romans 13:8, "Let no debt remain outstanding." Basic rules of Bible study, however, tell us we must interpret Scripture with Scripture. We cannot make any single text mean something that makes nonsense out of other scriptural injunctions. There are many scriptures giving instructions for lending, borrowing, and repayment. Romans 13:8 does not mean "do not borrow." It means make your payments on time, keep your contractual agreement, and do not default on your loan.

In Deuteronomy 15:1–3 Moses is giving instruction for a system of debt repayment in Israel. It is unlikely that any nation is going to use the application of a seven-year national cycle again, but remember our task is to extract the principle from the purpose this application accomplished. The principle here is that *debt is to be limited.* Israelites were not allowed to encumber people with debt in perpetuity. The system in Israel was universal. All of Israel's private debt was forgiven in the same year. If you borrowed in the first year of the cycle, you had seven years to repay. If you borrowed in the third year, you had four years to repay, and so forth. When the lender and the borrower entered into an agreement, they had to come up with a repayment plan that fit within the time.

My own country, the United States, has some of the best and worst examples of obeying this principle. Until the mortgage crisis in the early twenty-first century, when it came to buying homes, America had a wonderful system. The interest rate was required by law to be one of the lowest rates for any loan, and the mortgage repayment plan was for fifteen or thirty years. This system made the United States one of the largest private home–owning populations in the world. On the other hand, America's credit card system is more or less out of control. When you graduate from college, and often now even from high school, you get two, three, or even more unsolicited credit cards offers in the mail. Often pre-approved cards give you instant access to $1,000 to $5,000 of credit. Many people, young and old, use these cards without ever looking at the fine print where it says the interest rate is 19 or 26 percent. I have seen interest rates as high as 36 percent. If you follow the seductive plan and pay only the "small minimum payment" required, you begin to pay interest on interest and will pay back the original amount thirty or forty times. At one time this would have been called "loan-sharking" and would have been illegal. Today it is the norm for credit card payments in many countries. The problem of America's personal credit card debt is of major concern and undermines the stability of the nation's economy.

It would seem from the broad look at finances in the first five books of the Bible that lending was essential to enabling people to get out of poverty. The focus was on small business loans. The purpose of these loans was to get people out of need and able to provide for themselves. The goal was economic enablement. For generations Jews have continued to practice many of these principles. I have traveled to nearly half of the world's nations, and it is very rare to find a poverty-stricken Jew, even in very poor countries. That does not mean there are never poor Jews or that all Jews are wealthy, but they get established quickly and provide for themselves. Having an understanding of the purpose of lending, one Jewish family migrates and gets established. They send for the next family and loan them money to get started. That money is either repaid or is then loaned to the next family to come and get established. Lending, as Moses taught it, was about helping people get on their feet financially and become a productive part of the community. Lending was primarily a part of community responsibility and secondarily a way of making money.

I have been told about a Christian banker who studied these scriptures. He was distraught that in America the banking system is loaning to the wrong people, or perhaps it is better to say, is not loaning to the right people. US banking institutions tend to loan to the wealthy or to those who already have debt. But these same institutions will rarely approve a loan for immigrants, women, the unemployed, or the poor who have a plan for starting a business but have no capital but also no debt. This man began a private bank that loaned only to people who had a good idea for becoming a productive part of the community and only needed the money to get started. The bank has been enormously successful and has never had a defaulted loan. This is biblical economics.

Let's take another look at verse 3: "You may require payment from a foreigner, but you must cancel any debt your brother owes you." At first glance one could think that God does not care about foreigners as much as he cares about Israel. This is not true. Again, the apparent meaning here cannot be the accurate meaning because it makes nonsense out of many other scriptures. It is clear from Genesis to Revelation that God wants to bless all nations. This theme is so overwhelming that it cannot be contested. Then why didn't God require debt forgiveness for foreigners? The most probable interpretation of this variance is that the Jews were required to take the seventh year as a sabbatical year. They could not work nor could they work their animals or land. Therefore, they could not make payments that year. The non-Jews, however, were not required to obey this Jewish law.

They could continue to work and they could make payments. In fact, this was probably a windfall year for the non-Jewish immigrants, helping to enable them economically.

NO POOR AMONG YOU

Deuteronomy 15:4–5
However, there should be no poor among you, for in the land the LORD your God is giving you to possess as your inheritance, he will richly bless you, if only you fully obey the LORD your God and are careful to follow all these commands I am giving you today.

Verse 4 lays out a second principle we can glean from this passage. *Israel was to have a national commitment to the elimination of poverty.* Financial blessing came with financial responsibility within the nation. No teachings in Scripture give a limit to personal or national wealth. There is teaching that wealth should not be our life obsession, that we should not put our trust in wealth, that wealth can draw our hearts away from equally and more important things if we are not careful. However, Scripture also applauds financial initiative and the role of wealth in the blessing of the community. The Bible emphasizes that the economic system of the community is to be one that constantly addresses the elimination of poverty. For anyone to be poor and destitute in Israel was a shame on the whole community.

As I write this book in 2005, America is experiencing one of the greatest financial booms in its history.[4] Millionaires and billionaires are being created at a monumental rate. But the test of financial stability for a nation is not only the wealth being generated but also activity at the bottom of the economic scale. Are the poor increasing or decreasing? The United States has more billionaires and, at the same time, an increasing number of people who live under the poverty line. The problem is not wealth per se; the problem is the irresponsible making of wealth. The economic system of the Bible is not communist, promoting the idea that all resources must be divided up equally. Nor does it approve of disregard of the poor and the disenfranchised. Scripture promotes the idea that a growing and stable economic environment will be fostered, in part, by enabling those on the bottom of the economic ladder to move up and make their contribution to the quality of life in the nation.

In business more than in any other domain, Scripture emphasizes responsibility to the poor. Farmers were to set aside the edges of their fields so that the poor could work the gleanings. Managers were encouraged to make work for the less fortunate in the community. The church is also given responsibility for the destitute, but government is rarely mentioned in relation to its responsibility to the poor.

AID VERSUS DEVELOPMENT

For centuries Christian and non-Christian humanitarians alike have promoted the obligation of *nations that have* to help *nations that have not*. Not a bad idea, in the main, and one that has a great deal of biblical support. However, much of the application of this idea, both at the community level and the national level, takes the form of giveaway programs. The idea is that if those who have give some of what they have to those who have not, the poverty problem will be solved. On the surface this appears logical. In practice it is devastating and counterproductive. It actually produces poverty. The basic thinking is not biblical.

The Bible emphasizes opportunity over aid. Aid is reserved for those who have absolutely no way of providing for themselves and will die without assistance. Israel is certainly in this circumstance in the wilderness, and God provides for them. However, the day they stepped into the Promised Land, the aid stopped. The day they had the ability to provide for themselves, God withdrew the manna. They had no more money the day the manna stopped than they did the day before, but now they had opportunity to provide for themselves. God did not want to create a dependent people, but a people who drew on the gifts, talents, and resources he had given to provide for themselves. Here again we see that enablement is a major theme in biblical economics.

In everything that God does with Israel, he is working not only on their external circumstances but also on their internal view of themselves and of God. He wants them to become self-reliant, not dependent. He wants them to see what they are able to do, to create, and to build. He is working to develop their self-image and character as well as their economy.

This leads us to the next principle.

NO NATIONAL DEBT

Deuteronomy 15:6

For the LORD your God will bless you as he has promised, and you will lend to many nations but will borrow from none. You will rule over many nations but none will rule over you.

Israel was told not to borrow. *As a nation they were to have a policy of no national debt.* In order to understand God's reasoning here, we have to ask what a no-borrowing policy would produce in a community. First, they would have to learn to live within their means. Their wants would have to be balanced with their needs. Secondly, they would have to look into themselves as a people and learn what they were capable of doing, making, and discovering. In other words, they would be pushed toward self-reliance and away from dependence as a community.

In twentieth-century India, Indira Gandhi fostered a national program called "Buy India." The basic idea was to put a moratorium on imports, forcing India as a nation to learn to produce the things that they wanted. If India wanted cars, washing machines, video cassette recorders, televisions, and the like, then India was going to have to learn to produce them. The first cars, VCRs, etc., did not work very well. But they continued to improve. India slowly decreased the build-up of trade imbalance, increased employment, and developed a great sense of national pride in their ability to produce and provide for themselves. They moved farther away from dependence and toward self-reliance. God has gifted all peoples and nations, and part of his objective in discipleship is to see those gifts shine.

WICKED ECONOMICS

Deuteronomy 15:7–10

If there is a poor man among your brothers in any of the towns of the land that the LORD your God is giving you, do not be hardhearted or tightfisted toward your poor brother. Rather be openhanded and freely lend him whatever he needs. Be careful not to harbor this wicked thought: "The seventh year, the year for canceling debts, is near," so that you do not show ill will toward your needy brother and give him nothing. He may then appeal to the LORD against you, and you will be found guilty of sin. Give generously to him and do so without a grudging heart; then because of this the LORD your God will bless you in all your work and in everything you put your hand to.

Again we see that God knows the human heart, that humans are fallen and will not necessarily do what is right—not even his beloved Israelites. Remember, when this was written, they were still in the wilderness, having just spent four hundred years as slaves. God warned them that if he was going to bless them financially, they had to think about more than themselves. He wanted to bless them, but that blessing would come with a responsibility to the greater good of the community.

Notice in verse 8 the operative word *needs*: "lend him whatever he needs." Some Christians today think we have an obligation to give whatever anyone asks for. This is not a biblical mind-set. In fact, it works against biblical principles because it can produce laziness and dependence. Notice also the word *lend*. Lending is not the same as giving a handout. Lending is help to get started or to offset a crisis. It implies a relationship of accountability, enough involvement in the recipient's life to assess their need and ability to pay back.

A FEW PRACTICAL EXAMPLES

A Swiss friend told me a wonderful story of community responsibility. Her family lived in a tiny village that had one collectively owned vineyard. When a village family fell on bad times, they would be given this vineyard for one or two years. The family in need worked the vineyard and kept the produce from that season. When they had reestablished themselves, the community would pass the vineyard on to the next needy family. This kind of generosity and community responsibility is foundational to biblical economics.

While I was teaching in a missions school in Denmark, a Danish worker told of what she and other Danish missionaries had done with the Tibetan tribe with whom they work. This particular nomadic tribe had lost high numbers of yaks during several extremely harsh winters. Because the yak is the centerpiece of their survival, the tribe was in danger of starvation. So the Danish missionaries raised money in the West to help the tribe. They bought yaks and gave them to the most desperate families.

The missionaries asked me, "How did we do in applying biblical economics?" My response was that they had half a revelation—and half a revelation is better than no revelation at all! The team had seen that bringing the salvation message alone was not enough. They had to be involved in other areas of the Tibetan tribe's desperate needs. They saw a financial need and sought to address it. The problem was with their solution.

I asked one of the missionaries, "What would happen to the tribe if they had another series of harsh winters?"

She responded that they would be in trouble again. Exactly! The solution had not solved the problem. In fact, the solution had made the tribe more dependent, because now when they were in similar trouble, they would go to Danish missionaries for help.

"What can we do?" she asked.

Part of the problem was the focus on *we*. God, in his great heart to see a people developed, wants more emphasis on *them*. First of all, the tribe needed to be involved in making decisions. The goal of biblical economics is independence and self-reliance. With blessing comes responsibility, which must be one of the goals of the solution. What possible solutions were there? The tribe may have decided to take the yaks and to give one yak back after they had two calves— simple loan repayment allowing the missionaries to loan a yak to another needy family. Or the tribe may have wanted to set up its own system whereby it took responsibility and agreed to pass a second calf on to the family in greatest need. This would increase self-reliance and responsibility for the blessing. It would also begin a multiplication process of the original gift. Or again, the tribe may have decided to take the new yaks, sell every other newborn, and set up a "disaster relief fund" for future bad winters. Then self-reliance, responsibility, and long-range planning would be built into the tribe's thinking. That would be biblical economic discipleship.

A Swedish friend, a businessman, told me another wonderful story. While on business in a major African city, he was awakened in the middle of the night. He could not get back to sleep and felt that God was urging him to go for a walk. As soon as he stepped out onto the street, little boys selling candy surrounded him. They slept on the street in hopes of making a chance night sale. These children were destitute; every penny counted. The businessman struck up a conversation with the boys and with one in particular named David. He asked them how they lived, and discovered a tale of poverty, near starvation, homelessness, and slavery. The boys' owner gave them candy and sent them out into the street to sell it. They received 15 percent of their sales. This income barely kept them from starving.

My friend found that the value of their box of candy was approximately fifteen American dollars. He told the boys that he was a Christian and a follower of Jesus and that Jesus cared about their condition and wanted to help them. He asked David whether he could live better if he sold his own candy and kept all the profits. The boy responded that he would have more than enough. My friend made a proposal to the boy: He would give him fifteen dollars to buy his own candy. When David started making extra money, he would save it. When he had fifty dollars, he would help the next boy buy his own candy, and that boy would then do the same, and so forth. David's eager positive response was clear. My friend gave David the fifteen dollars and left.

Some months later a letter arrived in Sweden with news from David. All the boys my friend had met that night now owned their own candy. All the boys had enough to eat and places to stay. All the boys were now Christians, going to church, and helping other children get off the street. This is biblical economics: generosity, self-reliance, independence, responsibility, and multiplication all in one.

SUMMARY

We are just skimming the surface of what the Bible has to say on these subjects. Remember, the purpose of this volume is only to get us started thinking about and studying the Bible in new ways. We will have to do a great deal of homework before we are ready to articulate a biblical view of economics from the whole of Scripture.

Here are the economic principles in Deuteronomy 15:1–10 that we looked at:

1. Limit personal debt.
2. Eliminate poverty.
3. Avoid national debt.
4. Address legitimate needs of the poor.

The Hebrew mind could not grasp a concept of spiritual blessing without a tangible manifestation. The goodness of God was tied, in part, to having enough food, clothing, and shelter. The Hebrew word *shalom* (peace, wholeness) contains the concept of material blessing. Most of the earth's population today is desperate for this holistic gospel.

STUDY HELP

- Themes to consider when studying and coloring economics in the Bible: *ethics and principles of finance, loans, agriculture, the worker, labor, the manager, inheritance, wages*
- The domain of economics reveals: *Jehovah Jireh, God our provider*
- The primary attribute of God revealed in economics: *goodness*
- God governs this domain through: *the laws of agriculture*
- The color I used: *green*

WORKING VOCATIONAL MISSIONS STATEMENT

To develop an economy where needed goods and services are provided for the community along with gainful employment at a fair market price and wage.

Great issues include honest gain, enablement of the poor, integrity of the work force, stewardship of resources, and community conscience.

A NOTE TO ALL BELIEVERS

We all deal with finances and material blessing, or the need of it. This is not a travesty; this is not a terrible diversion from more important things; this is God's plan for revealing himself as Jehovah Jireh, the Lord of provision and goodness. So many want God's material blessing without understanding God's financial principles. God does want to bless us, but he wants to bless us in every area of our lives, not just provide us with material things. He wants us to be a blessing, not just to be blessed. He wants to bless us in ways that make us more like himself.

Do you know and live by God's financial principles? Can't answer that question? Don't beat yourself up; you have much company in the body of Christ globally. Do you want to know God's thinking about finance? Why not begin by reading his word with this theme in mind? I guarantee that God is ready and willing to disciple you in this area. You have to give him the opportunity by being in his Word. You are a part of God's strategy for discipling your community and nation. Will you step up to the call?

A NOTE TO THE BUSINESS PROFESSIONAL

If you are a banker, business person, laborer, manager, store owner, stock broker, or ditch digger who provides goods and services for your community or nation in any way, you are part of God's plan to reveal Jehovah Jireh, God our provider. The Bible has as much to say about finance and its purpose in blessing a people as about any other subject in Scripture, including salvation. Most view business today as a means to make money and nothing more. In Scripture business is a means to make money and a great deal more. It is about provision, about quality of life, about demonstrations of goodness and blessing. The Bible speaks about work as worship, about skill and craftsmanship being worthy of the Creator of work. The creature reveals the Creator in the quality of his work, just as the Creator has revealed himself in the quality of his work. Community responsibility and creative solutions reveal the goodness of God to every level of our society. You have a call of God on your life. Like Joseph, you are part of God's revelation of his ability to provide all that is needed in abundance. You are part of his plan to reveal the qualities of God through the quality of your work. What would happen if every Christian in the world showed up for work on time? Performed at their absolute best? Set their sights on blessing the community and company rather than blessing themselves? What would happen if every Christian who owned a business asked, "What does our community really need, and how can we provide that and still make a profit?" rather than "Where can we make the most money?" Before we can begin to dream, we must know what God wants us to dream. And in order to know that, we must understand what he has already taught us in his Word. Does something stir in your heart as you read this? Are you one called of God to begin saturating yourself with the mind of Christ and applying it in your life and work? You are part of God's strategy for discipling your nation.

CHAPTER 8

SCIENCE AND
TECHNOLOGY

If you listen carefully to the voice of the LORD your God and do
what is right in his eyes, if you pay attention to his commands and
keep all his decrees, I will not bring on you any of the diseases I
brought on the Egyptians, for I am the LORD, who heals you.
EXODUS 15:26

God saw all that he had made, and it was very good.
GENESIS 1:31

George Washington Carver was a black American former
slave who used his great mind to pull himself from bondage, becoming one of America's greatest scientists. He held over
one thousand patents for the use of the peanut alone. Asked how he
could think of a thousand ways to use the peanut, he replied that he
held the peanut in his hand and said, "God, you made every seed-
bearing plant, and you said they were good. What did you make the
peanut for?"

Many astronauts who has ventured out into space have returned
to earth talking about the Creator, awestruck by the magnificence

of the cosmos. King David and King Solomon were not only great political leaders, but they also loved science and worshiped the Lord of creation.[1] For the Jews, creation was the first revelation of God. Paul said the material world so eloquently reveals the invisible attributes of God that no one has an excuse for not believing in him.[2] Paul argued with the mystics of his day that God is not only the God of the unseen world but also of the seen.[3] It has been argued that modern science came from the biblical view that God created everything there is and that he created it with laws by which it works. The discovery and understanding of those laws can lead us to a better quality of life.

Today, however, many Christians loathe the discipline of science, thinking it is the battleground for disproving the existence of God. Others feel it represents the lesser plane of the *material* and not the more important *spiritual* realm. Some actually believe that it shows a lack of faith to search for and use scientific discoveries. These ideas are a far cry from the teaching of the Old Testament, the fruit of the early church, and the root of both Jesus' and Paul's messages. An understanding of the message of Christ that does not embrace the material world is more mystical than it is biblical.

The biblical message of "cleanliness is next to godliness" resulted in improved sanitation and health in history. The lower mortality rate of the Jews during the Black Death in Europe led some to believe that the Jews had magic arts, when in fact they were just continuing to practice what God had taught in the books of Moses. How does this compare with a "Christianized" southern Africa that is faced with near extinction because of disease? When some of the most important moral issues in the twenty-first century are being asked in the realm of science, what does the near absence of a clear biblical view forewarn?

Let's begin to get an idea of what Moses was teaching:

Deuteronomy 23:9–14
When you are encamped against your enemies, keep away from everything impure. If one of your men is unclean because of a

nocturnal emission, he is to go outside the camp and stay there. But as evening approaches he is to wash himself, and at sunset he may return to the camp.

Designate a place outside the camp where you can go to relieve yourself. As part of your equipment have something to dig with, and when you relieve yourself, dig a hole and cover up your excrement. For the LORD your God moves about in your camp to protect you and to deliver your enemies to you. Your camp must be holy, so that he will not see among you anything indecent and turn away from you.

The Scriptures are down-to-earth and deal with life at its most basic level. God deals with every dimension of his creation. Topics that make you and me uncomfortable are brought up for common-sense understanding. This passage in Deuteronomy begins by dealing with nocturnal emissions. We will spare the men and skip that and take up verses 12–14, which embarrass everyone equally.

God has brought a great deliverance for more than two and a half million Israelites and alien slaves. They have experienced the miracle of the parting of the Red Sea. They have been eating miracle manna dropped from the sky on a daily basis. But they still have to use the bathroom. You could say that this scene in the wilderness is the juxtaposition of God's teachings on the material world: he can invade our creation and do what none of us understands, but his daily norm is to work with the natural laws. In these verses God is teaching basic hygiene.

The principles are fairly straightforward. First, the community is to take responsibility for the daily need of all its citizens to urinate and defecate. Second, the citizens are to take personal responsibility to follow those guidelines. Third, the waste is to be buried, as opposed to put in the water or left on the ground. Fourth, the highest possible motivation is used—God's presence. God, through Moses, is teaching public health. He is teaching sanitation and preventive health measures. The same God who did the impossible for his people by parting the Red Sea wants to teach them about his material world and the laws by which it works, and he wants them to take responsibility for what they have learned. He is discipling them.

THE UNCLEAN SCRIPTURES

When I was growing up, the "unclean" scriptures were taught allegorically as parallels for sin. (And I was glad that I had not lived in Old Testament days, because walking through the streets shouting, "I am unclean," and spending a day outside the camp seemed fairly heavy treatment for minor infractions.) From the allegorical treatment one got the notion that women were more unclean than men. I think this was drawn from the teaching that the mother was unclean for more days after the birth of a female child than after the birth of a male child.[4] This concept of women being more unclean became tied to the idea that Eve sinned first and, therefore, women are more prone to deception than men. However, the "unclean" scriptures are not allegories; they are historical. More importantly, they are pragmatic guidelines given by God for community health.

The following list of everything in the books of Moses that would make you unclean is revealing:

- Touching anything taken as spoils of war.[5]
- Touching a human bone or grave.[6]
- Touching or being in the presence of a dead body.[7]
- Touching the discharge of a woman's period.[8]
- Touching the discharge of a man's semen.[9]
- Touching a man with a bodily discharge or his spit.[10]
- Touching the bed or saddle touched by a man with a bodily discharge.[11]
- Touching the nocturnal emission of a man.[12]
- Touching human uncleanness, meaning urine or feces.[13]
- Touching anything that touched any of these things.[14]
- Touching the bed or chair that a woman with her period had touched.[15]
- Touching or having a skin rash or outbreak on the skin.[16]

- Touching or being exposed to mildew.[17]
- Touching the blood of the sacrifices, if you were a priest.[18]

This list teaches us many things. First, it would appear that men are more likely to be unclean than women. Second, it seems that the poor priest is going to be the most unclean of all. Third, none of this is about matters of the heart. It is about hygiene. God is teaching community health and prevention. When he says, "If you obey my laws, you will have none of the diseases of the nations that surround you," he is not giving some formula for spiritual magic. He is teaching the prevention of transmittable diseases. And he is teaching this nearly 3,800 years before humanity will discover the germ. Not until the late seventeenth century would we learn that there are invisible microbes and viruses that can be transmitted from one thing to another and cause disease. We would not understand clearly until the 1990s that the most viral transmitters of these invisible enemies are bodily fluids. It has taken the AIDS epidemic to reveal the extent of God's advanced understanding.

In certain demographics in 80-percent-Christianized Africa, one out of four people, even one out of three, is HIV-positive.[19] What would the statistic be if we added in all the other infectious diseases taking lives in that region? Where is the biblical influence that produced the healthiest, most scientifically advanced nations of the world? Remember, when the gospel came to Europe, Europeans were the "filthy pagans" that the advanced Middle Easterners weren't sure they wanted to mingle with. Where did antiseptic Switzerland, Germany, and Scandinavia come from? The minds and then the cultures of these peoples were transformed by a gospel that not only dealt with the conversion of the soul; the gospel they received dealt with all of life. It was a gospel that brought physical health as well as communion with God.

George Kinoti says, "Africa is plagued by numerous diseases. The most important are infectious diseases, which are both curable and preventable. An obvious example is malaria, which causes untold suffering in Africa and claims something like a million African

lives a year. Malaria was once a major disease in the warmer parts
of Europe and the USA, but improvements in the living conditions
led to its disappearance."[20] Two-thirds of the world is crying out for
this gospel. Who will go? How will they know if someone does not
tell them?

HEALING

A young mother of two children under four sat across from me in a
New Zealand restaurant. She had just discovered that a dreaded lym-
phoma cancer had reappeared in her body just months after thinking she had been cured. The prognosis was not good. She looked at
me and asked, "What do you think of healing?" Everything in me
wanted to give popular charismatic or evangelical answers such as,
"By his stripes you are healed; claim it and believe for it."[21] I wanted
to give her the happy-ending version, but I had been studying the
Bible too long, and I knew that is not all that it teaches. Scripture
does not teach that if we believe in Christ, we will never get sick,
that if we believe, we will be healed or that we will never die. You can
find individual scriptures that would seem to mean that, but that is
not what they mean because they make nonsense out of many other
scriptures. Jesus died, and Paul had a physical ailment that God did
not heal even though Paul prayed three times.[22] Lazarus was raised
from the dead, and then he died again.

With a heavy heart I said to my friend that the Bible makes it
clear that miracles are possible, but they are exceptions, not the rule.
Miracles are spectacular interventions of God for his own unique
purposes, but they will never be the norm. We may always pray and
ask God for healing, but the gospel is that in death the enemy of our
souls is finally defeated, not that we will not die. We live in a fallen
world where disease is a reality. Our mortal bodies are wasting away.
We can learn to live more wisely and deal with disease with prevention and treatment, but we will all die. Then what is our hope? Our
hope is that, through his death, Christ has overcome the evil one.
At the very moment that Satan feels he has conquered us, the point

of death, we are given an immortal body not corrupted by sin. The cross has removed the sting of death, not death itself. The book of Job reveals to us that the enemy of God can sorely try us with crisis and illness, but it also reveals that Satan cannot take our life when we belong to God.

The thinking of many Christians today is that there should be no suffering, there should be no death, and we should have heaven now. Quoting Dr. Kinoti again: "Religion . . . enables many to evade reality. Christians . . . sometimes use their faith as a narcotic to evade the pain, the ugliness, the difficulties, the concrete reality of the world in which we find ourselves."[23] The author is speaking specifically about African believers. But this is not only an African problem. This is one of the great problems in evangelical, Pentecostal, and charismatic thinking in the last century and a half. We have drifted toward a belief that salvation delivers us from living in the material world. And it does not.

As I left the restaurant with my suffering friend, I longed to say something that would comfort and that was also true. I put my arm around her and said, "Here is what I do know. If you live, you will become pure gold through this trial. If you die, you will go into his presence and be perfected into his likeness. Either way, you cannot lose!" The week I was preparing this chapter I attended her funeral— knowing I had given her the comfort of his Word.

WORSHIP AND THE MATERIAL WORLD

All through Scripture, creation draws the hearts of God's people to him. David was stunned by the God who created the innumerable stars. Solomon tried to grasp understanding of the seasons and the God who created the rotation of the planets. Paul expected people to understand the existence and attributes of God simply by considering the creation around them. Creation captures God's awesomeness. In the era of cathedral building, Europeans were mystified by the nature of space. Because they could not yet define the molecular structure of things, air was mysterious and awesome.

They incorporated this into their worship by getting architects and engineers to invent new building technology to convey the awe and wonder of God's creation in their cathedrals. They understood that science and worship could work hand in hand. Millions still visit these great monuments every year.

Of all the domains, science is in a sense the most limited, because the scientist cannot discover anything that God has not created. Certainly scientists can have theories that are not based in fact. But scientists cannot create new laws or new truths in the cosmos; they can only discover them. Today many Christians believe, or at least behave as if, by virtue of our faith we are alienated from all scientific pursuit. This can be a grave danger. In the sixteenth century the church and science were at odds with each other. Galileo supported the Copernican theory that the earth was not the center of the universe. The theology of the day was built on a geocentric model, the idea that man and the earth were fixed at the center of the universe. Galileo was suspected of heresy and put under house arrest until he died.

In this instance science was right (to a degree), and the theological view of the day, based on a literal interpretation of certain scriptures, was wrong. God, of course, knew the truth all along. He was not thrown by our discovery. Science's discovery of some fact in his universe did not destroy the validity of Scripture or challenge God's truth. This discovery simply led to a clearer understanding of what God meant by man being the center of the universe. It revealed that humans are central to God's plan but not central in cosmic geography. God is not shaken by scientific discovery. He is not alienated from *his* material world; he uses it to reveal himself, and man is still discovering him in it.

King David was overwhelmed by the innumerable stars. He saw God revealed in the scope of what he could see. When I saw the Hubble Space Telescope's pictures of the birth and death of stars, I was awestruck. The color, the power, the majesty in the creation of just one tiny star; explosive plumes millions of miles high! I am humbled to think that I live in the first generation that God has graced with such a view of the beauty of his universe. The Hubble was aimed at a black spot at the end of the handle of the Big Dipper for ten days, absorbing light from deep space. When astronomers looked at the picture that the telescope sent back, they counted ten galaxies, each larger than ours, in the one black spot! Who cannot worship the God of creation when they see and discover such things? And yet today, with split thinking being the norm in the church, if I hear from Christians about the Hubble Telescope's discoveries at all, it is in the light of how the money could have been used for evangelism.

SUMMARY

Are you beginning to get the picture of what we have lost in Scripture? Are you seeing the tragedy of keeping God so boxed in? What else is God going to reveal to us in his universe? What other advanced understanding of the material world is he waiting to impart to us for the prevention of disease and beyond? God is the same yesterday, today, and forever. God has not changed; we Christians have lost our understanding of God. He wants to restore us, to revive us through the revelation of himself in the material world. Will we let him?

We have looked at one small passage dealing with sanitation. There is so much more: teaching about ecology and our responsibility to steward his creation, about cures, about the priestly role in primary health care, about the pharmaceutical properties of plants. When I see all that there is to study in the Bible, I must conclude that God loves science.

STUDY HELP

- Themes to consider when studying and coloring science in Scripture: *health, nature, hygiene, medicine, engineering, technology, ecology, animal kingdom*

- The domain of science reveals: *the Creator*
- The primary attributes of God revealed in science: *order and power*
- God governs this domain through: *the laws of nature*
- The color I used: *blue*

WORKING VOCATIONAL MISSIONS STATEMENT

To discover and use God's laws for the blessing of all people, pursuing a higher standard of living, better health, and better stewardship of all God's natural resources.

Great issues include prevention of disease, discovery, and stewardship.

A NOTE TO ALL BELIEVERS

God is not afraid of science or discovery. Neither should you and I be. For me, a balanced approach to biblical healing is as follows:

- Confess all known sin.
- Bind the enemy.
- Do everything medically known that may be helpful.
- Pray for a miracle.
- Put yourself in the loving hands of the Father; he knows best.

I can support this approach from the Word of God. I would ask God to reveal a cure to his science professionals, just as he revealed preventives of infectious disease to Israel. Which do you think is the greater lasting witness: a miracle for an individual, or a cure for everyone? Perhaps we cannot fairly ask that question, because both reveal God. Are you praying for *both* revelations—miracles and cures—for the nations?

Are you prepared to refuse skepticism about all science and let God speak to you through what he is allowing us to discover? Humans are fallen and tend to corrupt anything that can be corrupted. Cloning, for example, could lead to attempts to duplicate humans. But cloning and DNA research could also lead to a cure for many common diseases. Can we not see this discovery as the hand of God extended to us in mercy? The story of the tower of Babel is often used to discuss the evils of technology. But the sin of Babel was really political imperialism; the tower was just the symbol. What we see in Scripture is that when the technology got out of hand, God destroyed it by confusing the people.

What is the point for us then? Don't fret about new discoveries and developments. If they threaten God's plan, he will deal with them. If he is allowing the discovery, our question should be, "God, how do you want to use this to glorify yourself?" Christians did this with the discovery of movable type and the printing press. Yet some Christians push aside the technology of the Internet as demonic. What has changed? God? No, we Christians have. Alienation from discoveries which God is allowing can only result in lessening the purposes of God in our lives. Let's receive the whole counsel of God's Word in this wonderful arena of science and his material revelation.

A NOTE TO THE SCIENCE PROFESSIONAL

When I spoke on this topic in Urbana, Illinois, a sanitation engineer, whose brother was a missionary, came up to me in tears. All his life the work of his brother had been applauded as a *spiritual* calling. This man had been made to feel less important because of his *unspiritual* profession. He said to me, "No one has ever told me that what I do is important to God too."

I was in 40-percent-Christian Togo some time ago and saw that people had taken to spray painting, "Ne pas uriner ici!" ("Do not urinate here!") on the walls around their houses and businesses. I thought, *Great! Half the gospel of sanitation. But who will teach them the other half—where they should urinate?*

Several summers ago a large tribe of Pentecostal Gypsies came to Switzerland to hold healing and evangelistic services. They pitched a giant tent very near my home and used the parking lot of our forest running and exercise course for their cars and trailers. The two small toilets for the exercise course and their trailer toilets were obviously not adequate for the needs of such a large group. As the week's evangelistic services went on, the forest trails became increasingly littered with feces and toilet paper. Before judging, we needed to have compassion. These dear people had been taught that Jesus saves and Jesus heals, but they had never been taught what the Bible says about sanitation.

As a professional in the science domain, you have a high calling. You are the discoverer and steward of God's material creation. You are called to know him in a special way as he reveals himself in the things he has made. You are called to use that knowledge to bless individuals, communities, and nations. No calling in God's kingdom is second-rate. No domain of revelation is more or less important than another; each is created by God to reveal himself. The pastor has one job, and you have another. The missionary prays to be shown worthy of his or her calling, and so should you. God makes his cause-and-effect relationship with humanity most evident in this domain. He uses his natural laws to humble us and to reveal his awesome power and wisdom. Are you one of God's George Washington Carvers? Are you called to hold in your hand something of God's creation and say, "God, you made this, and you said it was good. Why did you make this peanut, atom, DNA, planet, bug, or tree?" The sky is not the limit. God's revelation of himself stretches to the farthest reaches of the cosmos. How far is that? Perhaps he will use you to reveal that to us and strike us with awe again. You are part of God's strategy for discipling all nations.

CHAPTER 9

CHURCH

The LORD had said to Moses: "You must not count the tribe of
Levi or include them in the census of the other Israelites. Instead,
appoint the Levites to be in charge of the tabernacle of the
Testimony."
NUMBERS 1:48–50

The reason I left you in Crete was that you might straighten out
what was left unfinished and appoint elders in every town, as I
directed you.
TITUS 1:5

Here is a trustworthy saying: If anyone sets his heart on being an
overseer, he desires a noble task.
1 TIMOTHY 3:1

All the Israelites were Jews, but not all Jews were priests. Under
God's direction Moses chose Joshua to continue political leadership while Aaron and the Levitical tribe were given the priesthood. From the earliest days in the wilderness God made it clear

that government and the priesthood were two distinct institutions, both with clear kingdom purpose and function. This concept of an ecclesiastical structure with an independent function, apart from the overall function of the body of believers, has been hard for Protestants to grasp since Luther nailed his treatise to the Wittenberg door in 1517. But understanding the institution of the church is foundational to understanding the unique, God-given functions of all the domains in society.

Today we use the words *priesthood, believer, body of Christ,* and *church* rather interchangeably. All Christians are priests, believers, and part of the church, the body of Christ. For clarity in this study, we need to differentiate between the people, the building, and the individual believers who work full-time in a particular function such as pastor, missionary, or evangelist.

When Luther highlighted that we are all part of the priesthood of believers, he did not mean that there was no structure or leadership in the church. (Under Luther's leadership and those who followed him, a church structure was created with pastors, elders, and deacons.) He meant that we do not need a "priest" to represent us to God. Because of the work of the cross and Christ in our lives, we are all now free to come before God ourselves. All believers are encouraged to fellowship on Sundays. However, some of us go to work on Monday at the same building where we went to church.

All of Israel was taught to be holy, but the Levitical tribe (the priests) were to model holiness to the rest of the nation. The book of Leviticus focuses on their unique role.

APPOINTMENT OF THE PRIESTS

In Numbers 1:47–50 the selection of the priesthood is a completely different process than that for choosing political leaders. In Deuteronomy 1:13 God instructs Moses to have the people choose their political representatives. In the development of the priesthood, God made the selection himself. The anointing to minister in the ecclesiastical order comes directly from God.[1]

The priests were not chosen on the basis of personal merit.[2] God made priests of the entire Levitical tribe. This is not to say that character and virtue did not matter; Scripture is clear that God desired a holy priesthood. But God did not choose the virtuous elite; he chose an entire tribe filled with every level of character and virtue. What was God's point in selecting this way? Was he emphasizing that no one is holy? That he was able to make anyone holy? That holiness belongs only to him, and no one is innately worthy of representing his holiness? We don't know all the answers, but this fact is clear: God sovereignly selected ecclesiastical ministers.

As Israel moved around the wilderness for forty years, they began to acquire things. Carts were divided out to each of the tribes. The Levites were given very few carts, and the Kohathites, who carried the holiest implements of the tabernacle, were given none at all.[3] They were required to carry the tabernacle and all of the utensils of worship and sacrifice on their backs. Over and over again God encouraged them to be satisfied with their unique inheritance in the Lord. The result of not being given carts, and additionally being required to carry the tabernacle, put a limitation on the priesthood's ability to acquire wealth. That did not mean that they were to live in destitution, but it did limit their potential for financial power among their people.

The priesthood was to receive its provision from offerings and was given small plots of land for farming in each of the tribal territories.[4] These directions made the priesthood uniquely dependent on the people to whom they ministered. They had all authority to speak for God and to represent him to the community, but they did not have total authority, for God had limited their financial and political power in the community.

The priesthood was not given territorial land.[5] On leaving Egypt there were thirteen tribes in Israel. Both of Joseph's sons, Ephraim and Manasseh, were given tribal status by their grandfather Jacob. As Israel formed government and began to prepare for their future in Canaan, God made it clear that only twelve tribes would have territorial or tribal land. The thirteenth tribe, the Levites, would have their inheritance in God. This meant that the priests would never need to form a government as the other tribes must. It also meant that the Levites did not need to develop an army as all the other tribes were commanded to do. The Levites were to be split among the other twelve tribes and territories and be God's priestly representation to all of them.

The priests were the first primary health care givers.[6] Until the scientific community developed, the priesthood took care of the primary health care needs of the people. If people had an infection, they were to go to the priest, who was to put them in quarantine and inspect them again some days later. The priests taught the dietary laws, which were about nutrition and health. The priests prayed and took the needs of the people to God. The priests offered sacrifices for their sins.

The result of this was that the priests had to constantly deal in the pragmatic, material world of God's laws of nature and in the unseen world of God's sovereign intervention. God did not allow the Levites to develop a mind-set that the seen and the unseen world were secular and sacred, one under God and one under man. Every day, as God's representatives, they had to minister to the practical, physical needs as well as the needs of the inner person.

The prophets anointed kings, but they did not appoint them.[7] This is most clear in the process of Israel first wanting a king. Israel goes to Samuel, the prophet of the day, to consult God. Samuel consults God, and God says that this is not a good idea. But the priests and prophets do not control this decision—the people do. And finally, Israel decides that they will have a king in spite of the fact that this is not God's desire. God then tells Samuel to go and anoint Saul and pray for him, because if Israel insists on having a king, Saul is the man God wants them to choose. But Saul is not officially appointed king when he is anointed. Only the people can give Saul authority to rule. Saul wasn't appointed king until "all the people went to Gilgal and confirmed Saul as king in the presence of the LORD."[8] The same basic process took place in the selection of David and Solomon. The Levitical tribe had political influence, but it did not have political control. The authority of the priesthood, like the authority in every other domain, was limited.

The confusion of political authority and priestly authority resulted in severe consequences. Two examples of this stand out in Scripture. The first is the incident in 1 Samuel 13:1–13. Saul had been to war and had won a victory. He and his troops were waiting on the battlefield for the prophet Samuel to come and offer the sacrifice to God before they could return home. Samuel was delayed, and Saul grew impatient. Finally, Saul decided he would offer the sacrifice. When Samuel arrived, he asked Saul, "What have you done?" Hearing Saul's response, Samuel said, "Now your kingdom will not endure." Saul was not satisfied to be given political leadership by God. He wanted more power. He wanted priestly authority over the people as well, and he lost his kingdom for confusing the two God-given domains. We find a similar confusion in the life of David.

David loved God, and he loved to worship. He used his political power to help build up the priesthood and the tabernacle and also to prepare the way so that his son could ultimately build the temple. This support does not seem to be criticized in Scripture. However, on one occasion David confused his role as king and the role of the priest, with serious consequences. David had been appointed king in Israel and had successfully conquered Jerusalem and defeated the Philistines. An invading army had taken the ark of the covenant. In 2 Samuel 6 David decided it was time to take back the stolen ark. "David again brought together out of Israel chosen men, thirty thousand in all." David approached this task as a military endeavor. He used the might of the army and his political authority to bring the ark back, and God could not bless it. "When they came to the threshing-floor of Nachon, Uzzah reached out and took hold of the ark of God, because the oxen stumbled." When the man who tried to steady the ark dropped dead, David knew that God was not with this venture. He cried out, "How can the ark of the LORD ever come to me?" David stored the ark in the house of Obed-Edom and returned to Jerusalem in defeat. But the story did not end there. In the same chapter David went again to retrieve the ark. God had answered

David's question of how to move the ark.[9] This time he went with the Levites, who offered sacrifices every six steps and carried the ark, as Moses had commanded.[10] God made it clear that he gave that authority to the priests, not the king. Later, Solomon understood this distinction, and he summoned the priests to carry the ark.[11]

God did not give all authority in his kingdom to any one domain or person. The prophets were advisors to the king, but they were not kings. The priests had authority, but not all authority. The political leaders had authority, but it was different from that of the priests. Under God, they had to work together in a system of checks and balances.

All of Israel was to be holy, but the priests were to be models of holiness to the community. The book of Leviticus contains instructions primarily for the priesthood regarding how they were to live and how they were to conduct themselves. They had a unique role in the community, but they did not have the only God-given role.

SECULAR VERSUS SACRED

Our split thinking between the secular and sacred is probably revealed more in the ecclesiastical order than in any other domain. Today it is common among Christians to think that if you are really "spiritual," really "obedient" to God, you will be a pastor, missionary, or evangelist. Many Christians feel that all other vocations are less important. The end result is that the majority of Christians today are sitting in pews with no idea of what God has called them to do, expecting the pastor and church leadership to do everything. This was never God's intent. In God's design every believer has a role to play in reaching and teaching the community. The priestly role was unique, specific, and just one of many roles.

Jesus understood the importance of keeping each domain in its proper place. When he saw that the money changers had moved their business inside the walls of the temple, he threw them out. He did not say that money changing was wrong. He said that it had no place in his Father's temple. He emphasized the role of this ecclesiastical meeting place as a "house of prayer."[12]

If we are to see "every creature reached" and "every nation discipled," we must learn again the specific role of the ecclesiastical institution—pastors, elders, deacons, denominational leaders—and how it relates to the calling and authority of each of the other domains.

STUDY HELP

- Themes to consider when studying and coloring the ecclesiastical order in Scripture: *religious rituals, prayer, offerings, sacrifices, priests, worship, tithes, feasts, idolatry, covenants, the tabernacle, the temple*
- The domain of church reveals: *the Great High Priest*
- The primary attributes of God revealed in the church: *holiness and mercy*
- God governs this domain through: *his sovereign choice and anointing*
- The color I used: *gold*

WORKING VOCATIONAL MISSION STATEMENT

The ecclesiastical order is called to represent God to the people and the people to God, discipling all believers in the nature and character of God and his Word and applying this to the work and walk of faith; to facilitate the expression of that faith in the worship and sacraments of the church; and to be a moral model of God's absolute standards of truth.

Great issues include calling society to accountability to the Word of God.

A NOTE TO ALL BELIEVERS

Many Christians are sitting in the world's churches today wishing they had a calling to be a pastor or a missionary. They feel they would be more spiritual in these callings. Many feel that they are not called to be pastors or church workers because they are less worthy. All of this is the by-product of split thinking. It results from the idea that the "secular" is bad and the "sacred" is good. This is not biblical thinking. If you are called by God to give your working life to family, or government, or business, or science, or teaching, or arts, or communication, you are not called to a lesser vocation than ministry within the church structure. Your calling is equally from God, equally vital to that of those called to serve within the church.

Discipling the nations is a saturation strategy of getting the truth into the fiber of every layer of society through the lives of every believer. For too long we have put all the weight of the work of God on the shoulders of the pastor or church worker. It is time for us to bear our own weight. What has God called you to do in society? It is time to recognize the doors God has opened for our life work and determine to carry out our job as a calling unto God himself.

A NOTE TO THE MINISTRY PROFESSIONAL

Some of you in the ministry today will be relieved by what I have said in this chapter, and some of you will be threatened. The pastor and missionary in the twentieth century have been expected by many to be all things to all people. When we discuss "discipling the nations," some will think all the work is their responsibility. Some are hoping it will be. Whatever your perspective, I encourage you to pursue God for a clear revelation of a working job description for yourself and for each of your congregants. Only when the 80 percent of the body of Christ *not* called to the ministry of the church are released to do what God has called them to do can those of us in full-time ministry in the church begin to focus on our call.

Some in the ministry have asked, "Why are we talking about discipling the nations instead of doing it?" It is the responsibility of the "priesthood" to teach and clarify for the body of Christ what its job is. It is not our job to start businesses and banks; it is our job to teach and disciple business people and bankers in the full counsel of God

as it relates to their calling. It is not our job to run the government
and write the constitutions; it is our job to teach those who are called
of God into those vocations how to carry out their responsibilities in
accordance with the Word of God. It is not our job to be the father
or mother to every family but to teach the Father's way of parenting.
This is so clear and simple that I am sometimes flabbergasted by all
the confusion. Have we so bought into the secular/sacred split that
we are unable to conceive of the call of God on those outside the
ecclesiastical institution? We are not to bring all the domains under
the church structure; we are to send the body of Christ away on Sunday prepared to be Christ's ambassadors of wisdom in their individual and specific domain callings. If we are to launch a generation
prepared to see qualitative differences in not only their lives but also
their communities, we must reintroduce an adequate theology of the
laity as well as of the "priesthood." The institution of the church has a
pivotal role in discipling the nations, and we must understand what
our role is and is not.

CHAPTER 10

FAMILY

Honor your father and your mother, as the LORD your God has commanded you, so that you may live long and that it may go well with you in the land the LORD your God is giving you.
DEUTERONOMY 5:16

Take to heart all the words I have solemnly declared to you this day, so that you may command your children to obey carefully all the words of this law. They are not just idle words for you—they are your life.
DEUTERONOMY 32:46–47

Of all the domains in the kingdom of God, family is probably the most discussed and studied by Christians. We base political platforms on "family values," and yet rampant divorce continues—with no significant difference between the Christian and non-Christian population.[1] Why? Can the power of God save our souls but not restore our families?

Over this last decade of coloring the Scriptures by domains in order to understand God's thinking in every arena of life, nothing has more impacted my thinking than God's view of family, its influence, and its role in community at large. I do not have one key scripture to study here, but thousands address marriage, children, in-laws, conflicts, sexual conduct, inheritance laws, family and finance, family and justice, education, and much, much more.

HOME AND WORLDVIEW

Like communication and education, the domain of family provides the warp to the government's and church's weave. Family's influence touches everyone and everything. It is said that by the time we are four, we will have learned or established 80 percent of our view of life. By the time we enter school, we know whether we are good or bad, whether the world is safe or dangerous, whether we are bright or stupid, and whether other people are to be feared or trusted. We have learned a life strategy of asking questions or building defenses. We already know whether challenges are exciting or dangerous. Uninterrupted, we will continue to evaluate all of life and the world we live in through that grid of reality. In modern Christian terminology, we have most of our worldview in place before we ever leave home for school. To say it another way, in our first four years of life, parents and the home environment will give us the definition of reality that we will use all our lives.

An impressive example of the power of that home influence is the cultural landscape of New Zealand. This small island nation's population is divided between indigenous Maoris and immigrant Europeans. In many ways New Zealand's daily life is integrated in schools, shops, transportation, news and mass media, and entertainment, dress, and sports. However, the worldview and culture of the Maoris and the Europeans in New Zealand are as different as if they still lived half a world apart. How can this be? Where are these values and views of reality learned? In the home! From the family! With almost no intentionality!

In an age when we focus on almost everything but the family—movies, TV, music, school, friends—God puts his sights directly on the family as the most important influence in society. The biblical overview leaves you with an overwhelming sense that, for God, family is sacred and the most important building block of all he has created. No wonder the distortion in this domain is so great. The family is responsible for God's most cherished of all attributes: love.

SONG OF SONGS

Few topics get an entire book in Scripture, but love and the anticipation of marriage is one exception. When God gives something so much attention, we should do the same. Song of Songs celebrates the exhilarating highs and lows of emotional love and the anticipation of its physical expression in marriage. In a day when Christians are viewed as having a diminished view of sex, God clearly thinks sex is a good idea. The Song of Songs is a celebration of the joy, comfort, and pleasure of marriage. It is celebrated not only by the bride and groom but also by their friends and the community at large. The message could not be clearer on God's side: Love is good. Marriage is good. Sex is good. And family is good.

Genesis 1 and 2 set the stage for the importance of men and women working together. God says that it takes both the male and female to reveal the image of God, and he blessed them and family as his primary strategy for filling the earth with the revelation of himself.

Genesis 1:27–28
So God created man in his own image, in the image of God he created him; male and female he created them.

God blessed them and said to them, "Be fruitful and increase in number; fill the earth and subdue it. Rule over the fish of the sea and the birds of the air and over every living creature that moves on the ground.

By Genesis 3 we can see that the enemy of God has another plan, which results, first of all, in a separation of God and man and, second, in hostility and distrust between man and woman. The devastating results can still be seen today as God's sacred creation of family remains a primary battleground in every society in the world. Consider just two issues: divorce and abortion. Divorced men are more likely to suffer mental illness; divorce and separation are a risk factor in attempted suicide; and financial ruin and poverty follow divorce. In abortion the next generation is maimed before it ever has a chance at life. That's the bad news about family. What's the good news? What was God's intent in creation?

Our Western idol of individualism has nearly blinded our biblical scholarship to the importance of family and community. The idea that living completely alone would be paradise seems idyllic, but it is sterile. You cannot express love, justice, friendship, generosity, and wisdom alone on an island. God's most wonderful ideas and characteristics are revealed in how we live together, and we begin learning these attributes in the domain of family.

THE ROOT OF ALL CULTURE

As we follow the development of humanity through the Genesis narrative, we see that individual traits become multiplied and strengthened in families. Then, as families grow, those same traits become amplified into cultural, tribal, and finally national traits. Take, for example, Abraham's tendency to be manipulative, and sometimes actually dishonest, especially when it came to women in the family. In Genesis 12 Abraham deceives the pharaoh about the nature of his relationship with Sarai (Sarah) in order to protect himself. In spite of God's promises in chapter 15 Abraham allows himself to be talked into seeking an heir through a concubine, and so begins the story of Ishmael and his descendants (chapter 16). In chapter 20 Abraham is again faced with danger and lies to Abimelech about his wife. After Isaac is born and marries Rebekah, he carries on the family trait of lying about the nature of his relationship with his wife in order to protect himself from danger (chapter 26). Jacob enters the picture and, with the help of his mother, deceives Isaac as to his identity in order to steal Esau's blessing. Jacob flees to his family in Paddan Aram and meets his match in his uncle and future father-in-law, Laban. These two spend twenty-one years trying to get the better of each other over the issue of Rachel.

Are you beginning to see the pattern and escalation?

As Jacob flees Laban and resettles his small tribe in Shechem, personal character flaws, which have grown into destructive family patterns, explode into tribal disaster. In chapter 34 Jacob's daughter Dinah is violated by Shechem, a prince, who is remorseful and actually loves and is loved by Dinah. Jacob's sons, in the name of family honor and in order to obtain the wealth of the Shechemite tribe, deceive and then murder every male in the Shechemite tribe.

A character trait has run its full course into cultural identity and ends in genocide. This trait of treachery turns on the family and takes Israel into Egypt and four hundred years of exile and slavery. Joseph is given opportunity to respond in deceit when he is unjustly abused by Potiphar and his wife, the cup bearer, the baker, and finally, with great temptation, his own brothers. But he refuses to deceive and is used by God to save his family, his tribe, and his host nation from great famine. God is teaching us many things in Genesis, but certainly one of the major themes is the influence of individuals on families, families on communities, and communities on tribes. Discipling nations begins in the home!

FIRST LINE OF DEFENSE—VALUES

One of the first things that struck me in the study of family was the emphasis placed on time together for parents and children and how that time was to be used. Over and over again I read verses like, "Impress [God's commandments] on your children. Talk about them when you sit at home and when you walk along the road, when you lie down and when you get up. . . . Write them on the doorframes of your houses and on your gates."[2] These are instructions for parents in teaching their children God's thoughts on all of life, and modeling how these principles are to be lived out in daily life. Not only is parental responsibility and authority reinforced in Scripture, but government or church involvement in the primary discipleship of children is almost completely absent.

We hear much complaint about the lack of responsibility in our schools, our churches, and our entertainment industry to give children good values, but God puts the greatest weight of responsibility on the parents. I do not want to argue *for* immorality, violence, and drugs. However, when we blame the gun, the entertainment industry, the government, the schools, and the streets for our children's problems, we are not focusing on what God focuses on. In essence we are saying, "Make the world safe so that my child will be safe." This is far from the biblical view of reality. God says, "In order for your children to be safe in an unsafe world, teach and model what they need to know and understand. Sin is real, and you are surrounded by destruction. Teach your children to choose good over evil!"

Scripture indicates that this will take time and assumes that parents and children are doing things together and using opportunities to discuss how God's view of reality relates to everyday living. Can we really expect children to take these values seriously if they do not see them modeled and revered in their parents' lives? By the time they go to school, children know from the way their parents live whether honesty, justice, integrity, courage, and other character traits are important or not. Of course, teachers, pastors, friends, and culture can have a dramatic impact, but the home is still the formative influence and, in God's eyes, clearly the most important. It provides the grid of reality the child will use to interpret all other influences in life.

FIRST LINE OF DEFENSE—MORALITY

If we would just obey one of God's Ten Commandments, "You shall not commit adultery," we would nearly eliminate the following:

- rape
- incest

- pedophilia
- sex slavery and trafficking
- AIDS and venereal disease
- abortion

Overwhelming, isn't it? Today we seem to be shocked by sexual immorality. In the Bible God seems to take it for granted. Scripture teaches that human beings, if undeterred, will have sex with just about anyone and anything. How else do we explain the long lists in Deuteronomy and Leviticus on who (and what) not to have sex with? Somewhere we've picked up the idea that sexual morality is the norm and deviance is the exception. God seems to think otherwise in both the Old and New Testaments.

Look at just this one chapter:

Leviticus 18:5–24
Keep my decrees and laws, for the man who obeys them will live by them. I am the LORD.

"No one is to approach any close relative to have sexual relations. I am the LORD.

"Do not dishonor your father by having sexual relations with your mother. She is your mother; do not have relations with her.

"Do not have sexual relations with your father's wife; that would dishonor your father.

"Do not have sexual relations with your sister, either your father's daughter or your mother's daughter, whether she was born in the same home or elsewhere.

"Do not have sexual relations with your son's daughter or your daughter's daughter; that would dishonor you.

"Do not have sexual relations with the daughter of your father's wife, born to your father; she is your sister.

"Do not have sexual relations with your father's sister; she is your father's close relative.

"Do not have sexual relations with your mother's sister, because she is your mother's close relative.

"Do not dishonor your father's brother by approaching his wife to have sexual relations; she is your aunt.

"Do not have sexual relations with your daughter-in-law. She is your son's wife; do not have relations with her.

"Do not have sexual relations with your brother's wife; that would dishonor your brother.

"Do not have sexual relations with both a woman and her daughter. Do not have sexual relations with either her son's daughter or her daughter's daughter; they are her close relatives. That is wickedness.

"Do not take your wife's sister as a rival wife and have sexual relations with her while your wife is living.

"Do not approach a woman to have sexual relations during the uncleanness of her monthly period.

"Do not have sexual relations with your neighbor's wife and defile yourself with her.

"Do not give any of your children to be sacrificed to Molech, for you must not profane the name of your God. I am the LORD.

"Do not lie with a man as one lies with a woman; that is detestable.

"Do not have sexual relations with an animal and defile yourself with it. A woman must not present herself to an animal to have sexual relations with it; that is a perversion.

"Do not defile yourselves in any of these ways, because this is how the nations that I am going to drive out before you became defiled."

God could have saved an enormous amount of time by just shortening this to "don't have sex with anyone but your spouse." But God is defining what he means by the word *adultery,* and he is emphasizing the destruction of immorality, especially in the family. We must not think this means sexuality outside the family is not a sin, but God is stressing that sexual immorality within the family has multiple victims—the two engaged in sexual conduct, and the families that surround them.

Today, we in the religious community seem to highlight the destructiveness of prostitution and homosexuality while virtually ignoring marital adultery, sexual abuse, and incest, which are all rampant. I have never heard a sermon on incest or rape and its impact on family and society. I am not arguing that we should condone any destructive sexual behavior. I am simply saying that we have ceased to view the severity of these issues from God's perspective. We take adultery and divorce fairly lightly, even in the church.

How can we raise children who will be able to withstand the sexual onslaughts of the world if they do not see morality modeled in the home? How can we have bold, confident children when so many family secrets send a message that is contrary to what God says? How can we be shocked by what God takes for granted? And if we don't teach our own children to love and respect their bodies and to view sex as a godly and sacred act in the faithful covenant of marriage at home, then who will teach them? Please don't think they won't figure sex out until "it is time." As we confront government and school programs that teach sexual behavior, let us remember that God has given parents the responsibility to model and teach that value to their children. If they don't, someone will. God knows who should.

FIRST LINE OF DEFENSE—PROVISION

In both the Old and New Testaments, family is the first line of protection against poverty and economic ruin. The definition of *destitute* and who should feed the destitute was one of the early debates in the church. Paul makes it clear in 1 Timothy 5 that if the poor have family, the family is to take care of them.[3] Only if the poor have no other alternative (i.e., work or family) is the church to give assistance. The custom of the Pharisees was to tithe everything, even the herbs in their kitchen. Jesus rebuked them for tithing mint and neglecting to care for the needs of others.[4]

The book of Ruth recounts the story of the widow Naomi and her widowed daughter-in-law, Ruth. Refugees, childless, and without recourse in a foreign land, they return to Israel and the town of their family origin. Here they find aid by gleaning in the fields of their closest relative, Boaz, who takes his right as "kinsman-redeemer," marries Ruth, and brings her and Naomi into his home to care for them. What a wonderful concept, kinsman-redeemer! God's first line of responsibility for those in financial need is the family, not the church, community, or government.

Jewish culture, in general, still functions this way. As we observed earlier in the subject of lending, when Jews immigrate, a few from the family go first, get established, and then bring the next ones over and help them get established and so on. They may not be rich, but they are not in need and are rarely dependent on anyone outside of the family. This is not just savvy business; it's God's principle of family responsibility being lived out.

In today's independent world we focus on self-reliance. That is not entirely bad, but in Scripture God balances independence with family and community responsibility. Today's deteriorating view of family is contributing to the poverty of both the individual and the community.

FIRST LINE OF DEFENSE—JUSTICE

Deuteronomy 21:15–21 can be disturbing if we are reading it for application and not principle:

> *If a man has two wives, and he loves one but not the other, and both bear him sons but the firstborn is the son of the wife he does not love, when he wills his property to his sons, he must not give the rights of the firstborn to the son of the wife he loves in preference to his actual firstborn, the son of the wife he does not love. He must acknowledge the son of his unloved wife as the firstborn by giving him a double share of all he has. That son is the first sign of his father's strength. The right of the firstborn belongs to him.*
>
> *If a man has a stubborn and rebellious son who does not obey his father and mother and will not listen to them when they*

discipline him, his father and mother shall take hold of him and bring him to the elders at the gate of his town. They shall say to the elders, "This son of ours is stubborn and rebellious. He will not obey us. He is a profligate and a drunkard." Then all the men of his town shall stone him to death. You must purge the evil from among you. All Israel will hear of it and be afraid.

This passage is not a teaching for polygamy or capital punishment of teenagers. At the time Moses is writing these passages, the tribes are polygamous and violent. The guideline "eye for eye, tooth for tooth"[5] is already an attempt to curtail their vengeful justice system in which they take a life for a slap.[6] God has never been oblivious to the realities of the peoples he is discipling, and he is not unrealistic. Discipleship takes time, and a step in the right direction is a good step. An overview of Scripture clearly shows that monogamy is God's highest ideal, but the people are polygamous at this time in history, and within that less than desirable state of affairs, there must still be justice. The importance of this passage and similar laws is to show that family members, whether men, women, or children, have rights and that family members have a responsibility to honor those rights and carry out those responsibilities.

No record in Scripture tells of a rebellious teenager being stoned. I don't think that is surprising. The message of this passage is parental responsibility. Parents must invest the time and be responsible to discipline. If that is not effective, they have to bring the child to the leaders. It is the community's responsibility to weigh whether the parents have done all that is possible and if the child is truly incorrigible. Another passage tells us that the parents have to lead in applying the punishment. The principle is not that rebellious teenagers are to be stoned; the principle God is putting forward here is that parents *are* responsible for the actions of their children.

In the book of Esther we see a wonderful example of family responsibilities being carried out. Esther is an orphan and a refugee. Her cousin, Mordecai, raises her as his daughter. He is instrumental in her becoming queen of Persia. Mordecai modeled a passion for justice not only in his family but also in his community. When the pagan king—who holds the Jews in exile by force—is in danger of assassination, it is Mordecai who warns Esther of the plot and saves the king's life. Then Mordecai calls upon Esther to use her position as queen to save the Jewish people from a plot of genocide hatched by Haman, another political leader. Mordecai lived by the rule "love your neighbor as yourself"[7] and modeled it in caring for his family, his host country, and his own people. He understood that justice included loving your neighbor. His simple modeling of that to a family member, Esther, resulted in the saving of a nation.

Jesus says the whole of the law can be summed up like this: love God, and love your neighbor as yourself.[8] James calls this the "royal law" and goes on to say that showing favoritism in applying this law is sin.[9] What happens when children observe discrimination in their home? Parents speak of justice for strangers, but treat each other unjustly. A pastor preaches love on Sunday, but beats his wife. We talk of God loving the lost, but show intolerance of different ethnic groups or "types" of sinners. We constantly criticize our government, but don't even vote. How can we raise children to believe and model justice if justice is not modeled in the home? How can we hope to influence our communities if we do not model community concern and action at home? The answer: we can't. The family is God's first line of defense for individual and community justice.

FIRST LINE OF DEFENSE—LOVE

God summarizes the whole of his thinking about life in one word: love. God's definition of love means the presence of justice, provision, integrity, and truth. The authority behind government as God created it to function is the people. The authority of science is the unchangeable, God-created laws of nature. The authority of the church is its right handling of the Word of God. Authority in the family is expressed through love—love that is defined by the way Christ loved the church.

Ephesians 5:22–6:4

Wives, submit to your husbands as to the Lord. For the husband is the head of the wife as Christ is the head of the church, his body, of which he is the Savior. Now as the church submits to Christ, so also wives should submit to their husbands in everything.

Husbands, love your wives, just as Christ loved the church and gave himself up for her to make her holy, cleansing her by the washing with water through the word, and to present her to himself as a radiant church, without stain or wrinkle or any other blemish, but holy and blameless. In this same way, husbands ought to love their wives as their own bodies. He who loves his wife loves himself. After all, no one ever hated his own body, but he feeds and cares for it, just as Christ does the church—for we are members of his body. "For this reason a man will leave his father and mother and be united to his wife, and the two will become one flesh." This is a profound mystery—but I am talking about Christ and the church. However, each one of you also must love his wife as he loves himself, and the wife must respect her husband.

Children, obey your parents in the Lord, for this is right. "Honor your father and mother"—which is the first commandment with a promise—"that it may go well with you and that you may enjoy long life on the earth."

Fathers, do not exasperate your children; instead, bring them up in the training and instruction of the Lord.

The younger leaders I work with in ministry have a hard time with the fact that I still teach structure in the family. I am open and willing to listen to what these leaders have to say, but until I see their view in the Word, I have to withhold change in my thinking. As I look at the whole of the Bible, I see structure in every institution God has created. God designed the universe to function that way. I see family structure in Scripture. Parents have authority over children until they leave home, and husbands over wives. I know some hate to see those words; we have a knee-jerk reaction against them because the concept has been abused and made to mean things God could never condone. Many in history have abused Scripture in order to make themselves more powerful. But what is really meant by these texts that show structure and authority?

If we move this discussion away from who takes out the garbage and who does the laundry to who is responsible and when are they responsible, God's intention for family structure becomes clearer. For instance, if a spouse is unconscious in the hospital and needs surgery, who should be able to give consent? If a family member borrows money and fails to pay, who should be responsible? If a parent dies in an accident, who should get the children? Who should take financial responsibility for children until they are old enough to take care of themselves? The Bible is clear: God gives a great deal of responsibility to the family domain.

THE AUTHORITY OF FAMILY IS LOVE

So there is structure and authority in the family. Now, how is that authority to be carried out? When is the authority of family being abused and to be forfeited? When should a child be taken from a home? When must a spouse flee a marriage? When should the government take authority away from parents? How do we determine the difference between parental discipline and abuse of a child? Difficult questions! To answer them, we must ask another question. How do we define love?

Ephesians says love is demonstrated in the way Jesus works with the church and the way a person takes care of his or her own body. Love says, "You are as important to me as me." In fact, this kind of love says, "You are more important to me than me." The authority of Christ over the church was expressed by giving up his life in her service. He gave up his life that we might have life.

This is radical stuff. Husbands, this means that if you are to have authority in your marriages, you must be "chief lover." Your authority in your home is based on the quality of your love. Parents, to have authority over your children, you must love them. The less faithful your love, the less authority you will have with them. In fact, if you act in a way that is destructive to your spouse or children, you have no authority and they can and should be taken from you.

Should a spouse or child endure life-threatening abuse because God gives authority to that family structure? Absolutely not. God *never* gives all authority over all things at all times to anyone! He is the only one we can trust with that kind of authority, and he even limited his control over our lives by giving us free will. That freedom has rights and responsibilities for each of us. When anyone tries to remove that freedom entirely in the name of any authority, it is called tyranny.

To understand what Paul means when he teaches us to submit to the authority of government, look at how he lived out that submission. When the Roman government ordered him to stop preaching, he disobeyed their authority and willingly went to prison for it. There was a higher authority over his faith and actions: God himself. When the government exercised authority not given to it by the people or by God, Paul exercised civil disobedience. This subject is a book in itself, but my point here is that no one, including family, has all authority over anyone. Scripture teaches that to honor, submit, and obey does not always mean doing what we are told. This concept is probably most abused in the arena of family.

MYTHS ABOUT FAMILY

We have looked at numerous truths about family revealed in Scripture. Finally, let's look at destructive myths about family that are floating around some Christian circles.

Men Are over Women

Sorry, no such principle exists in Scripture. There is a structure that is particular to family, but there is no overall mandate of men having authority over women. In the Old Testament, Barak lost his military honors for not following the orders of his Commandress in Chief, Deborah.[10]

We Will Want Sex Only with One Lifetime Partner
Sorry again! The Bible seems to assume that we will have sex with just about anyone or anything unless we are taught differently. In the Old Testament God teaches sexual conduct in great detail (as we have seen), and in the New Testament Jesus teaches that temptations are common to all humanity and, furthermore, that he experienced them all!

Love Means Never Having to Say I'm Sorry
No! Love means the presence of justice, provision, protection, and harmony. "Love is patient, love is kind. It does not envy, it does not boast, it is not proud. It is not rude, it is not self-seeking, it is not easily angered, it keeps no record of wrongs. Love does not delight in evil but rejoices with the truth. It always protects, always trusts, always hopes, always perseveres."[11]

I Need Sex to Be Happy and Fulfilled
If that were true, surely we would be one of the happiest and most fulfilled generations in history. Scripture does say we need intimacy in relationships to be happy and fulfilled, but we can have that with or without sex. There is nothing more lonely than sex without intimacy and nothing more fulfilling than intimacy with or without sex. We must marry for the right reasons or we will continue to have marriages that fail.

Staying Together Is the Key
Staying married is less financially damaging and often better for everyone, especially children. But when we broaden the discussion to "why marry in the first place" and God's purpose for marriage, we can work on staying together for the right reasons rather than just bandaging a hemorrhage.

A Good Marriage Will Always Feel Good
Wrong! In God's design a good marriage will rub against both spouses' rough edges until they are smoothed into the image of Christ. Part of

the purpose of marriage is to help deliver us from ourselves by bringing us face to face with ourselves in a loving environment.

—⊶⊷—

STUDY HELP

- Themes to consider when studying and coloring the subject of family in Scripture: *wives, husbands, sons, daughters, children, widows, orphans, principles and ethics of relationships, sexual conduct*
- The domain of family reveals: *the Father*
- The primary attribute of God revealed in the family: *love/nurture*
- God governs this domain through: *the laws of love*
- The color I used: *orange*

WORKING VOCATIONAL MISSION STATEMENT

The purpose of family is to provide a safe, nurturing environment for growth and the development of values in the next generation. It is the smallest building block of human society.

Great issues include love, discipline, modeling God's thinking, preparation for vocation of the children, and the husband's love setting the tone of the home.

A NOTE TO ALL BELIEVERS

We all live in some form of family, and our first witness to the surrounding world is how we live in that context. We can accomplish nothing greater in our community or nation than what we accomplish in the microcosm of our own home and family. Our close relationships give us a mirror in which to see how much we are reflecting God's glory. Through family we see what God wants to work on in our lives to make us more loving, more like himself. This is an ongoing, lifelong process of growth. Each stage of life gives us opportunity to grow in new areas. God is there to help us. Childhood, adolescence, marriage, parenthood, middle age, grandparenthood, old age, illness, and death all give us opportunities to grow as individuals and families. This is called living, and with Christ it is called abundant living, being made more like him on a daily basis. Family is a sacred covenant meant to produce godlikeness in us all. When you grow here, you will take more of Jesus into everything you do and you will reproduce his likeness.

A NOTE TO FAMILY PROFESSIONALS

Whether you are a family counselor, family lawyer, social worker, or any other family-oriented professional, yours is one of the most important arenas in society. If the family is healthy, we will have healthy communities and healthy nations. It is so important that you see your work and the role of family from God's perspective. We must touch family structures very lightly and invade only in the direst of circumstances. However, we must not allow abusive injustice to rule in any family. When and how to step into a family unit to save the individual is a vital and delicate balance. Only God's perspective and wisdom can help us in individual cases and in making policies, guidelines, and laws that bridle our profession's authority so that it does not destroy the very institution it is there to protect. You have a wonderful and sacred call; fulfill it in the wisdom and power of his Spirit.

CHAPTER 11

EDUCATION

Fix these words of mine in your hearts and minds; tie them as symbols on your hands and bind them on your foreheads. Teach them to your children, talking about them when you sit at home and when you walk along the road, when you lie down and when you get up.

DEUTERONOMY 11:18–19

Love the Lord your God with all your heart and with all your soul and with all your strength and with all your mind.

LUKE 10:27

Education, like communication and the arts, is difficult to isolate and study apart from other areas in Scripture. Everything in Scripture is about learning. The Bible is a book inspired by God for our education and understanding of his ways. So, again, with this chapter we do not have one scripture that serves as an example; instead, we will look at a scriptural overview of the subject. God is a God of knowledge. He can be known. He wants to be known, and he wants us to know him in all that he has made. In a sense, inquiring minds are godly minds, and one of the primary marks of discipleship is expressed in the desire to learn and know.

WE CAN KNOW

Epistemology is a big word meaning the "science of knowing." All philosophies and religions ask, "Can we know?" and, if so, "How can we know?" God's Word says, yes, we *can* know! And we will know through a combined process of discovery and revelation. The basis of modern science—that the material world is real, measurable, and discoverable—is a biblical concept. The Islamic world can copy technology but has a hard time creating and maintaining it because of the belief that there are no fixed laws by which God governs the material world. There is only the will of Allah. Hinduism and Buddhism teach fundamentally that the material world we live in is not real and not important. Many Christians today hold doctrines that get dangerously close to this concept. But the Bible teaches that truth is discoverable and knowable and that truth, when applied, consistently results in the same consequences. God knows all truth, and all truth, in any and every domain of life, reveals God. Mystery in Scripture is a result of the difference between what humans can know and what God knows. Scripture shows that God originates and encourages wisdom, knowledge, and education.

EDUCATION REVEALS THE ATTRIBUTE OF WISDOM

For the Hebrew mind, discipled by the teaching of Moses, the concept of knowledge included *application*. This is far from most worldviews today. Most educational systems are based on the concept that you can *know* by retaining information about a subject without needing to apply it. As a result, many employers feel that university graduates can do nothing when they first come to work. They have to be taught *how* on the job. This greatly concerns educational professionals worldwide and has become a subject of debate and study.

This same idea—that data is knowledge—has led to a generation of Christians who say they know God but still don't know how to obey him. Many believe that they can *know* the Writer of Scripture without applying any of his principles; that they can be saved but not demonstrate any fruit of that conversion in daily life; that, as some say, they can believe like God and act like the devil. None of these are biblical assumptions. From Genesis through the book of Revelation, God reinforces the concept that knowledge is demonstrated in action, faith in works, learning in growth, wisdom in love.

There is, however, no scriptural basis for a "blind leap of faith." Existentialism says we cannot *know*, we can only *experience*. But Jesus refused to leap off the temple at Satan's temptation. He understood that we can know the will of God without taking the leap. The experience of leaping is not the only way to know. For God, wisdom is not just choosing right, but understanding why it is right. God's ultimate goal for us is not obedience but agreement. As parents we understand that in the beginning we must say, "No!" to a child who is about to put his little hand on a hot burner. We try to convey that it is hot and that he will be burned, but when he is small, we are satisfied if he just doesn't touch it. As he matures we are looking for him to become aware of what we mean by *hot* and, hopefully without permanent damage, begin to agree that burning flesh is a bad and painful thing. In the end we want him not to touch the burner because he agrees that it is not a good thing to do.

As we grow in God, we will need to ask about fewer and fewer things, because we will have learned God's thinking on those subjects. This does not mean we no longer inquire of God. It means we no longer ask God the same question, because we know and agree with his answers and reasoning. We will learn and ask God about things that are new for us because we do not yet have God's view on them.

The Old and New Testaments are full of admonitions to add to the experience of knowing God personally, to gain information about God revealed in creation, history, and the written word. Paul writes of renewing our minds and taking every thought captive and making it conform to the mind of Christ.[1] He encourages the church in Corinth to pray with their minds, with understanding, as well as in tongues.[2] In Acts the people of God were "one in heart and mind."[3] Paul warns of a sinful mind and admonishes the Romans to have a "mind controlled by the Spirit."[4] The entirety of Proverbs celebrates the blessings of wisdom applied to our lives and encourages the lifelong pursuit of "her." Over and over again in the books of Moses the Israelites are admonished to study and learn the ways of God revealed in the Torah (the Law of God) and to apply them to their lives. Jesus had mastered these principles by the time he was twelve and astounded the priests with his wisdom.[5] One difference between Jesus and the Pharisees was that they quoted the Law but he explained it. He understood it. He could apply it to daily life. Jesus calls his disciples to "ask, seek, knock," to inquire and learn of him and his Father. All of the prophets admonished Israel to turn back to the principles laid down by God through Moses and to see the blessing of God return.

REPENTANCE MEANS CHANGED THINKING

The New Testament word *repent* is often taught to mean "to change direction." The actual translation of the word from the Greek is "to change thinking." In other words, the key to changed behavior is changed thought, not the other way around. When we focus on actions, we become obsessed with the appearance rather than the substance of our lives. We *look* good, but we are unchanged on the inside. God's concern is not so much the external as who we are internally. God desires to win us to his view of reality and truth so that we are like him, seeing reality as he sees it.

In 2 Corinthians 10 Paul argues that our warfare is a warfare, in part, of the mind. "For though we live in the world, we do not wage war as the world does. The weapons we fight with are not the weapons of the world. On the contrary, they have divine power to demolish strongholds. We demolish arguments and every pretension that sets itself up against the knowledge of God, and we take captive every thought to make it obedient to Christ."[6] Our warfare with this world is a warfare between ideas, and a warfare to get a grasp of what reality is. If we are to stand and be an influence, we must not only act as Jesus would act, but we must think as Jesus thinks.

EDUCATION AND THE FAMILY

In an *Economist* article in the late 1990s, researchers wrote on successful classroom learning. They discovered that it had little to do with how much money or time was spent on the subject; less learning could take place when more time and money had been spent and vice versa. One determining factor for success or failure was the method of teaching. Parental support was another factor that educators worldwide agreed is important. If parents are involved in the child's education, the child will learn more. Scripture strongly agrees with this discovery, emphasizing the authority and responsibility of parents in teaching their children.

Deuteronomy 6:20–25

In the future, when your son asks you, "What is the meaning of the stipulations, decrees and laws the LORD our God has commanded you?" tell him: "We were slaves of Pharaoh in Egypt, but the LORD brought us out of Egypt with a mighty hand. Before our eyes the LORD sent miraculous signs and wonders—great and terrible— upon Egypt and Pharaoh and his whole household. But he brought us out from there to bring us in and give us the land that he promised on oath to our forefathers. The LORD commanded us to obey all these decrees and to fear the LORD our God, so that we might always prosper and be kept alive, as is the case today. And if we are careful to obey all this law before the LORD our God, as he has commanded us, that will be our righteousness."

Deuteronomy 11:19–21

Teach them to your children, talking about them when you sit at home and when you walk along the road, when you lie down and

when you get up. Write them on the doorframes of your houses
and on your gates, so that your days and the days of your children
may be many in the land that the LORD *swore to give your fore-*
fathers, as many as the days that the heavens are above the earth.

CHILDREN ABSORB THEIR WORLDVIEW

As we discussed in the chapter on family, in those formative years
from birth to four years old, when children absorb the view of reality around them, the parents' perspective is the critical factor. The
child *will* take in the values and beliefs that are modeled in the home,
whether they are intentionally taught by the parents or not. The
child will believe the reality parents convey and will copy it. Children have no choice at this stage of growth, because they are exposed
to no other reality. Parents will imprint their actual, not necessarily
desired, value system on the child. For this reason God emphasizes,
over and over again, the importance of parents teaching their children God's view of life in the everyday activities of eating, walking,
and working together.

I am not suggesting that Scripture indicates all parents should
homeschool. That is one method of education, and the Bible does not
put forth a single model. Based on their parents' influence, however,
children will go to school believing they are either smart enough or
too stupid to learn. They will enter school believing that learning is
either important and exciting or boring and a waste of time. When
they come home, the importance of homework will be reinforced
or devalued. Home will be a place that promotes learning or a place
that disrupts it. At home they will acquire the belief that something
can be learned from everyone and that everyone's ideas need to be
evaluated, or that there is nothing to learn from anyone. Before they
ever go to school, children will believe in a God who reveals truth,
or that there is no truth.

Have you ever wondered why God spends so much time on the
early life of Daniel and his training in Babylon? Daniel and his three
friends are captive aliens in Babylon, taken from their families as

adolescents into the palace and service of the king. They attend Babylon University, where they study witchcraft, divination, and other sordid subjects, and they are at the top of their class. They are surrounded by a pagan, idolatrous culture, yet none of them absorbs any of it. How do we explain this in a world where Christians and non-Christians alike are declaring television, movies, music, advertising, and schools to be the formative influences on young people's minds? How did Daniel and the others stand in this Babylonian environment? The answer is simple and profoundly emphasized in Scripture: they took their values with them. They continued to weigh the values around them in captivity with what they had been taught and, more importantly, seen modeled in their homes. Scripture indicates that if children are the victims of the world around them, there can only be one explanation. They are not being given the tools at home to evaluate the messages coming at them from the world, and they have not been given the confidence that they, with God's help, can know and discern truth.

EDUCATION AND GOVERNMENT

For several decades Christians in my country (the United States) have been very vocal about the damage to our public school system caused by the removal of prayer from schools. I do not want to argue for the absence of prayer, but I do want to discuss the thinking behind this argument. First of all, from God's perspective you cannot outlaw prayer; you can only outlaw prayer meetings and praying out loud. God has given no authority to government to rule over our hearts and minds. We can think and believe what we like. The institution of government can only attempt to control our outward actions. For decades we have traced the decline of our schools and education in the United States to a law banning prayer when law cannot ban prayer unless we agree to it. The law is unjust, but is it catastrophic?

On the other hand, something else took place in the United States that perhaps had far greater implications. The authority of education began to move consistently from parent- and teacher-based local organizations toward a national association for education. This shift in authority from family to government was far more strategic and dangerous than outlawing prayer meetings. God gave no authority to governments over our children. God gave that authority to parents. Governments are created by God to deal with the masses. By design, that is their function. Education, by its nature, is an individual process. Like social issues of poverty and drugs, if you ask the government to deal with it, you will have the most expensive and least effective programs. The government will design a program that attempts to deal with everyone in the same way—much like a prison system. But social problems, drugs, and education are individual issues that can only be solved effectively by addressing the individual. God designed the family to deal with individuals. Parents can delegate their authority to a public school system, but if parents abdicate their support or if their role is ignored or even denied by the institution, those schools have very little legitimate authority over the children. The same is true when parents abdicate responsibility for their child's education to a Christian school. God does not give the church the responsibility to train children. He gives that responsibility to parents.

EDUCATION AND THE HUMAN MIND

In education and in communication it is important to look at how God has created the human mind to work. Today's media culture emphasizes the power of persuasion to the point that we begin to think of ourselves more as sponges, taking in every message and conforming to it. When a crisis hits, we blame the impact of the media, or schools, or postmodernism, or the way youth think today. We talk about "secular" education as though it were a power in and of itself.

This is not the view of man conveyed in Scripture. In the Bible the human race is given great authority, the authority to accept or reject the influences around them. Nothing in God's Word indicates that it is easy to make our fellow man do what we want. Far from it. Scripture emphasizes humans' ability to accept or reject influences around them. In the next chapter, on communication, we will discuss brainwashing, subliminal communication, and the "recordable man" theories. But for the sake of our discussion on education, let me summarize by saying that once we move on from those very formative first years, we learn what we want to learn. We are far more like filters than sponges. This is so profoundly true that Communists in the former Soviet Union drummed doctrine into schoolchildren for seven decades and yet no more than 20 percent of them believed in Communism. Generations of black children in South Africa were taught that they were to have no role in the political life of their nation, yet almost none of them believe it. Maori and European children in New Zealand attend the same schools and come out with incredibly different worldviews.

Educators I've talked to all over the world agree that the two most important keys to learning are the parents' attitude and involvement and the child's motivation. The biblical view is that every child is gifted, every child can learn, every child has value, and every child has the right to reach his or her full potential. But the Bible also emphasizes that we are created by God to be free and we make choices whether to hear (learn) or not. The greatest influence on those choices will be the first few years in our home environment.

Why do I emphasize this? Because we have to recognize what an education system can and cannot do. We have to realize the importance of parenting. We have to give schools their proper place in God's scheme of things, but not expect them to work miracles or work in isolation. And we have to put our hope for the future in more than education.

STUDY HELP

- Themes to consider when studying and coloring the subject of education in Scripture: *teaching, learning, remembering, mind, thought, reason, nurture, wisdom, and family*

- The domain of education reveals: *the Great Teacher-Rabbi*
- The primary attribute of God revealed in education: *wisdom*
- God governs this domain through: *the laws of human nature*
- The color I used: *brown*

WORKING VOCATIONAL MISSION STATEMENT

To provide for the development of the God-given gifts in every child for the service of their fellow man and society, believing every child is gifted by God and has the right for those gifts to be developed to their highest potential.

Great issues include value-based integrated process with family involvement and support.

A NOTE TO ALL BELIEVERS

Do you love learning? Are you interested in everything? God is behind all learning and knowledge! If we are to model Jesus to those around us, part of that modeling will be his passion to know his Father in every area of life. One of the most tragic effects of the split gospel is the loss of interest in the world and in thought and culture. Often it seems that the only thing a believer can talk about is church, prayer, heaven, and hell. Not that those are not important. But, were Jesus here on earth today, he would be ecstatic to be in the first generation of humans to see through the Hubble Telescope a star being born or dying. His Father created the stars, and Jesus would praise him for all that the heavens are still teaching us. He would stand in awe at the way his Father created the DNA of the human species. He would ponder the fact that every cell can reproduce every other human cell and what that says about the nature and character of God. Jesus would love the idea of going to other planets and discovering more of what the Father has made. He would be reading, listening, eager about what is going on in his Father's cosmos and he would be excited about what we are learning and how God wants to use that insight.

God has made us with the capacity to learn (or refuse to learn) and to know (or refuse to know). From Genesis to Revelation God portrays himself as the Lord of knowledge, revealed in all the truths of the universe. Choose to think like God! Choose to be interested. Model Jesus' love of learning, and you will make those around you hungry for more.

Children love learning unless they are taught to be afraid of it. All it takes to learn is willingness to admit you don't know. That is the humility of a child. Children naturally ask questions. They have to be taught to feel foolish about the eagerness to know things. God loves questions and calls us to "ask, seek, knock"—and become like children again.

A NOTE TO EDUCATIONAL PROFESSIONALS

Wherever I speak on this subject, educational professionals ask me what they can do to influence their education system. The first thing I tell them is to study God's Word until they believe they see learning from God's perspective. Zeal without wisdom is not good. Secondly, whatever their job or position, they can seek more parental involvement. Teachers can communicate with and seek communication from students' parents. They can organize parental dialogue about the school system and their classroom. In many countries parents can be invited to volunteer and add to the curriculum and classroom management. How teachers involve parents is not as important as believing that it is essential. The critical thing is to understand God's principles. The applications will be dynamic to our community's specific situation.

I love the story Bruce Olson conveys of his experiences with the Motilone Indians in South America.[7] This tribe had Stone Age practices and was almost entirely isolated from the outside world when Bruce went to live with them. An amazing movement of God took place among these people, and the entire tribe was converted to Christ. As they grew in God and began to understand the importance of Scripture, they believed they needed to tackle the issue of education and learning to read. Rather than imposing a system on the Indians, Bruce Olson asked how they wanted to go about the process of education. The tribe decided that the elders needed to learn to read first so that they could teach the children, otherwise the fiber of authority in the tribe would be destroyed. If the elders learned first, the importance of learning would be enhanced and they would be able to model for the children the value of reading. What a great application.

Administrators and school board members should seek influence and policy that brings back parental involvement and authority in our school system. This is not to say that government does not have a role in organizing and overseeing an educational system. It is to say the system must base its authority as much as possible on parents and local institutions. As a principal you can create a voice for parents, whether in a formal or informal way. You can create a communication strategy that helps parents feel informed and involved, and you can help your classroom teachers do the same. I do not mean to imply that getting parents involved is an easy task. Apathy abounds. But the more parents are involved, the healthier the school system will be.

CHAPTER 12

COMMUNICATION

And God said, "Let there be light," and there was light.
GENESIS 1:3

Do you have eyes but fail to see, and ears but fail to hear?
MARK 8:18

I have called you friends, for everything that I learned from my
father I have made known to you.
JOHN 15:15

O f all the domains, communication is the most difficult to isolate and study. The Bible is made up of books, poems, and
letters through which God intended, along with everything else he
made, to reveal himself. He is the Word. The visible world reveals his
invisible attributes. Mankind is made in his image. The Holy Spirit
leads us into all truth, and Jesus reveals the Father. Everything God
does is communication, and everything you and I do communicates.
We are communicators made in the image of a communicating God.

One great difference between biblical thought and all other world-views and religions is that Scripture reveals God seeking to communicate with and redeem man, while others help man seek and find God.

Again, we have no single text for this domain, because the entire Bible is communication, but we will look at an overview of the subject.

God compares himself to words. He calls himself the living Word and says that words have power if we give them power. As much as any other arena, the domain of communication reveals the sovereign will of God's human creation and our individual ability to listen to, see, believe, and say what we like. God will not overrule that sovereignty of the individual, even for his own message. We have the power, we have the right, to accept or reject anyone's ideas, concepts, or words. Our job as Christians is not to overpower others with our view of the world, but to persuasively communicate our message—to give others a choice so that, by the grace of God, we "might save some."[1]

WE ARE SOVEREIGN

God is sovereign, and, created in his image, we are sovereign. What are we sovereign over? We are sovereign over ourselves. We should not sin, but we can sin. God does not desire to be separated from us, but we can choose to separate from him. We do not have to spend eternity in heaven; we can accept or reject the truth when it is presented to us. When we study communication and the domain of the individual, we see the power of sovereignty and just how wonderfully, and terrifyingly, we are made.

Research reveals that we have the ability to see and hear what we want to see and hear. We filter out messages that we reject or that make us uncomfortable. For example, some family members of alcoholics simply cannot see the pattern of abuse, because it is too painful. Whole groups of people can be invisible in a culture, such as women in Afghanistan or Indians in America. I see this every year in the productions of our communication students' videos. Whether Asian, black, islander, or white, students fill their pieces with their own kind. No matter the dominant race on location, they film those who are like them because that is whom they see.

This difference of perspective is so predictable in human society that if two or three witnesses in court testify to seeing exactly the same things, the testimony may be thrown out. The court assumes that the witnesses have collaborated on their testimony. We have such a powerful sovereign will that we rule over the messages we receive and reject.

TODAY'S VIEW OF COMMUNICATION

The view of communication and influence held by many non-Christians and Christians alike is the opposite of what God stresses in his Word. We claim that culture, family, and individuals are being destroyed by television, movies, music, and mass media. But God says in his Word that he has placed authority with the individual; he has given his human creation the power to choose.

If communication media were powerful in and of themselves, evangelism of the world would be simple and cheap; we could just broadcast God's Word from every street corner, television, and radio in the world. The power of the media would overwhelm people, and they would be converted. But, in this scheme, as soon as converts were exposed to a different message, they would be unconverted. If Christians switched the channel from a Christian program to an atheist program, they would convert to atheism. Of course, this is ridiculous and I am being facetious, but that is a fair conclusion to this exaggerated sense of media power. The media are not powerful in and of themselves. They are an influence that we, the audience, choose to empower or not. God clearly conveys in his Word that power on earth rests with the individual. Why? Because that is the way God made us.

Does that mean content doesn't matter? No, not at all. There is good content and bad content, good quality and poor quality. But at the end of the day, people have watched and listened to what they want to be influenced by. The popularity of a given message is a reflection of the audience, not the power of the message itself. Words have power, but not the power of control; they have the power of influence. We have embraced unbiblical thinking when we make the message more powerful than the person. God desires that we use our eyes to see the difference between deception and reality, our ears to hear the difference between lies and truth. When we embrace this as the way God created us to function, we can embrace our role as communicators who offer people a choice.

TRUTH IN A FREE FORUM

If we are to think like God, we must be more concerned with what is *not* being conveyed through the media than what is. We get so busy trying to silence those who disagree with us that we fail to notice that the truth is not being conveyed. We worry that the Internet is proliferating pornography and forget the printing press did the same thing. The Gutenberg press that helped create a revolution in printing the Bible also created a revolution of smut. Technology is neutral. It multiplies the message, good or bad. So, for what "good" are we to use the Internet? What alternative are we giving those who are surfing the Web? The problem with the media since the invention of the television is what is missing rather than what is there. Are there choices? Can the truth be found? That is our responsibility as God's people.

We can see this in the life of Jesus. If you study the New Testament carefully, you will find no documentation of Jesus silencing anyone—except demons, and they were all speaking the truth.[2] Jesus made no attempt to stifle the voice of the Romans, the Greeks, the Zealots, the Pharisees, or any of the hundreds of messages flooding his region of the world that he did not agree with. All were given free rein to continue disseminating any message they believed in. Jesus did, on the other hand, safeguard his right to continue freely bringing his message until he knew it was time for his arrest.

The absence of righteousness and truth in others' messages was not a concern to him. He focused on the freedom to bring his message into that open forum. God was giving people a choice, not demanding control of what they were hearing. Truth in a free forum speaks for itself. God is not interested in hiding evil. He is interested in our comparing light to darkness and making a choice between the two. The absence of righteousness means people have no choice. Rather than spending all our energy on silencing those we disagree with, we should spend time making our message available. Scripture indicates that the light has even more impact in darkness.

DEVELOPED VERSUS UNDEVELOPED

These principles of communication, applied to communities and nations, produce interesting evidence. Not *one* developed country today is without a free press. Perhaps more striking, not one undeveloped country *has* a free press. It would seem that the freedom to express ideas is tied directly to people feeling responsible for their societies. It is true that with a free press lies can be told and freedom abused, but the truth can also be told and people can make a choice.

Christians who believed in the right to communicate began the first newspaper in the United States. The masthead of that paper read, "To Cure the Spirit of Lying." The only thing needed to bring salt and light to a free nation with a free communication system is someone willing to tell the truth. And if we want to secure the right to a free forum for our own message, we must defend others' right to speak.

THE MEDIUM IS NOT THE MESSAGE

Christians were ecstatic when Gutenberg first invented movable type. Printing could now put inexpensive Bibles in the hands of believers. The use of this technological innovation by the church was such a revolution that Christian publishing became the largest segment in the industry. As newspapers evolved, Christians were in the forefront. The Salvation Army produced the first feature-length movie. Christian communicators had such passion for the use of radio that Christians at one time owned more radio licenses world-wide than any other single group.

But with the emergence of television, computers, and the Internet, Christians' thinking on media changed dramatically. Rather than seeing new technology as an opportunity for making the truth known in new ways, some saw it as a threat and perhaps evil in itself because of its potential to carry destructive messages. This shift in the view of communication has resulted in a near absence of any significant contribution to these media. The early leaders in the US film industry were self-governing, and religious leaders were automatically included in review boards. Christian leaders pulled out of this "secular" arena rather than being asked to leave.

Today, God has given us the greatest communication technologies in the history of humanity, but how much vision or passion for the use of these new media do we have? A negative view of technology is not biblical. All scientific discovery is morally neutral; only the use of it can be classified as good or evil. If we do not repent of our wrong thinking in this area, the "age of communication" may be known in history as the darkest age of all.

THE IMPORTANCE OF WORDS

Throughout the Old Testament and into the New, the importance of words is dramatically emphasized—whether in relation to promises and vows, testimony and bearing witness, treaties and agreements with other nations, or our accountability before God for every word.

There is no more dramatic difference between developed and underdeveloped nations than their view of words. We are flabbergasted as we watch leaders from other regions of the world swear on television that there is no invading army, even as tanks roll in behind them. At first glance we think that is just arrogance or stupidity, but it is far more significant than that. People's ability to say something unrelated to apparent facts is tied to two beliefs: one, there are no objective facts—*truth* is whatever god wants to be true; and, two, words mean nothing. In a worldview where god is the *only* reality and there are no checks and balances to that reality, words cannot communicate reality. We mean nothing, and our words mean nothing.

This is very close to the postmodern idea of "reality is anything I believe it to be." It is impossible to overstate the importance of the biblical influence of reality and truth of communication on the development of justice, science, economics, and general quality of life. Our entire concept of contracts, testimony, agreements, and relationships is built on the importance and the validity of our words. Much frustration in dealing with global cultures results from our failure to realize that this view of communication has not been part of the building blocks of these worldviews. Part of "teaching the nations" is laying a biblical foundation of communication.

STUDY HELP

- Themes to consider when studying and coloring the subject of communication in Scripture: *the use of the book, poetry, history, speeches, scribes, messengers, the tongue, words, scrolls, tablets, monuments, writing, signs, storytelling.*
- The domain of communication reveals: *the Living Word*
- The primary attribute of God revealed in communication: *sovereignty*
- God governs this domain through: *the laws of human nature*
- The color I used: *red*

WORKING VOCATIONAL MISSION STATEMENT

To provide truthful, objective information of importance to the community at large, so that citizens can make informed decisions.

Great issues include freedom of belief and therefore freedom of speech, proclamation, and preaching; the right to assemble; vows, commitments, covenants, witness, testimony, and remembering; and the written word.

A NOTE TO ALL BELIEVERS

I always get quite an audience reaction with this teaching on communication. Parents argue that they don't want their children exposed to everything that is out there; others ask if I am defending everything that is on TV and in movies. I get questions about record burning and library standards for the community. Much of this is put forth with a great deal of emotion.

As parents or responsible adults caring for young children, we have to set a standard for what is good and what we approve of, and what is "premature" for a child to be exposed to. We have the right and the responsibility to do this. However, we must also prepare the child for young adulthood, when he or she will no longer be protected by others and may be exposed to almost anything. If our discipleship results in confidence and discernment in young adults, then, like Daniel's parents, we have done a good job. If it results in fear and the need to live insularly, then we have failed. Rather than teaching people how to be in the world and not of it, we will have produced religious hermits who cannot be in the world at all. Christians cannot be salt and light in hiding.

What this means is that we must teach our charges to be discerning of the communication that will come across their path. We must teach them to interpret the message, discerning the thinking behind it. What is biblical and what is not? We must also teach them to discern the character and motives of the communicator, even if the message itself is true. Would they be able to discern that it was demons who cried out to Jesus, "You are the Son of God" and "I know who you are—the Holy One of God"?[3] Jesus could. This is the discernment we want to multiply.

In our zeal to improve the Web, movies, television, and the over-all communication industry and environment, we must not deny so many rights that we lose our right to speak through the same media. As we defend our right to speak, we must defend others' rights as well. I think it is fair to ask, Would Jesus have been allowed to preach at all in a Jerusalem controlled by orthodox Pharisaism? Did the paganism of the Romans contribute to a freer environment for the preaching of the gospel? We must not support any movement that seeks to drastically limit a free forum of communication within a nation.

A NOTE TO COMMUNICATION PROFESSIONALS

I led a public relations project in Washington, DC, in the 1980s. At the time, my media friends estimated that out of approximately seven thousand journalists working there, twenty or less were Christian. In some ways it seemed more acceptable among evangelicals to be a prostitute than a journalist. At least prostitutes were candidates for salvation; journalists were perceived as the "enemy." Things have improved, but media is still a ripe field ready for salt and light.

I have worked with thousands of young people over the last three decades who want to become communication professionals. Because of the environment they have grown up in, they tend to define Christian media work as preaching on TV or radio. It is as though we are unable to think of a purpose in media beyond evangelization and church. This is the by-product of split thinking. I often ask people what a "Christian" wheel would look like or what a "Christian" pilot would do. They have a hard time defining these. That is because we have made a false distinction between "Christian" and "good." The very thing that makes a good pilot "good" is already biblical, whether we realize it or not. If we take it a step further to news, entertainment, documentary, or any other area of communication, what should the truly Christian version look like? Are you part of the generation who will find out?

CHAPTER 13

ARTS AND ENTERTAINMENT

He has made everything beautiful in its time.
ECCLESIASTES 3:11

One thing I ask of the LORD, this is what I seek: that I may dwell
in the house of the LORD all the days of my life, to gaze upon the
beauty of the LORD and to seek him in his temple.
PSALM 27:4

Everything that God has made is beautiful. Nothing in the
universe is without color, form, and design. God turns ashes
into beauty. He is our Song and Potter.[1] The arts reveal the Creator
through music, words, color, design, balance, movement, harmony,
rhythm. David said that the stars sing the glory of the Lord, and
some physicists today believe that the planets do in fact vibrate in
perfect harmonic chords.

On the seventh day of creation, God rested. We should not think
of this rest in terms of tiredness, because God does not suffer fatigue.
We should think of it as his taking time to contemplate the beauty

of creation and savor the goodness of all that he has made. The arts reveal God's beauty, rest, and celebration, and his purpose for this domain is to renew and restore us and give us joy from our labor.

A CHRISTIAN ARTIST OR AN ARTIST WHO IS CHRISTIAN?

Christian artists today have a terrible conflict in understanding the purpose of their gift. If their work does not talk about Jesus directly, does it still have value? Can they work on productions with non-Christians? When some see a magnificent building, painting, or play or hear a wonderful performance, they are tempted to ask, "Was it produced, created, and performed by Christians?" as though that would validate the beauty. But beauty, in and of itself, is an attribute of God. Putting a Jesus sticker on it does not make it more beautiful. Preaching may be beautiful, but beauty does not necessarily preach an additional message. We may have art and beauty in the church, but to reveal God, art does not have to relate directly to ecclesiastical expression.

Anything can be used for good or evil. There are no such things as demonic musical notes, rhythms, or instruments. Satan does not own these any more than he owns the moon or mushrooms or color. All these things are an extension of God's creation. Anything that God has made may be used to worship Satan, but it can also be used to reveal God. Some Christians think of old music as godly music, and anything new is suspect, if not evil. This has more to do with personal taste than God. We happily listen to the beautiful Lutheran hymns, content that this music reveals spiritual virtue. What most of us don't know is that Luther put Christian words to the beer-garden favorites of the day. I wonder how the German Christians of his day responded to those popular songs being used in church.

MUSIC IN SCRIPTURE

Three types of music are recorded in Scripture: worship, national or political music, and love songs. One entire book, the Song of

Solomon, is a love song. Today worship music (hymns, praise songs, and psalms) is important to us, but we have lost the importance of celebrating human love and love of nation. If you look at the national anthems around the world, you will find that the vast majority of them written before 1970 mention God and his blessing. Before then it was largely understood that God is involved in the political life of a nation. In the last century some nations have sought to remove these references to God. Is that because of the secularization of the country or the church's loss of the understanding of God in the political arena? Also, where are the love songs? Our airwaves are crammed with a message of love that is demeaning or lewd. But today, when a musician who is Christian writes and performs a beautiful celebration of human love, we accuse him or her of being "secular" or not loyal to faith and not presenting Jesus. Yet Scripture celebrates all these themes of music and uses them to reveal God.

If we define opera as a story put to music, then Moses gives us a very early, if not the first, opera in Deuteronomy 32. It is amazing to think that this national political leader so understood the importance of music in the life of a nation that, at the end of his life, he would compose a work containing important principles for the people to remember. Moses recited the words of this song from beginning to end in the hearing of the whole assembly of Israel.[2]

THE DISCIPLINES OF THE ARTS

As with science, God rules the arts by laws that govern each discipline; laws of aesthetics, harmony, rhythm, dissonance, color, form, design, positive and negative space. Whether dancing, sculpting, painting, writing, or composing, every artist and performer understands that there are principles upon which their discipline is built. Mastering those fundamentals is foundational to their skill. Genius, then, is making those same fundamentals disappear in artistic expression. Unredeemed people create beautiful things because they are created in the image of God. They just do not realize the source of their talent or discipline or their love of beauty. They do not know the Gift-giver, but their gift still celebrates God. They are unaware of whom to be grateful to. Whether or not artists know God does not make their creation more or less beautiful. Beauty has intrinsic value as an extension of God's character and nature.

CELEBRATING ARTS AND ENTERTAINMENT

So much of what is called Christian music and art today is mediocre at best. Perhaps this is because we think the only thing that matters is whether our music talks about God. It is important to present the message of Christ. However, it is not only absurd but it is danger-ous to think along these lines. Is the only important thing about a surgeon his love of God, and is his technical skill in surgery unim-portant? The heart of the individual and the discipline of a craft are two different things, and Jesus is Lord of them both. As people who believe in the creator God, we are to value skill as well as right stand-ing with God. We are to celebrate beauty for beauty's sake because the Lord is the Lord of Beauty, the Creator of all skill. We are to seek the artist's right relationship to Christ, the creator of his gift.[3]

There are no tribes, nations, or cultures without art, music, and sport. Beauty, song, and celebration are all pre-human; they were expressed in God before we existed, and they still reveal him. We don't have to justify our love of sports or art by turning it into an opportunity to talk to the person next to us in the stands about God. We may or may not find that appropriate. It's okay to enjoy talent and God-given gifting for their innate value. It is worship of the Cre-ator, the Gift-giver, and a celebration of who he is!

———⚮———

STUDY HELP

- Themes to consider when studying and coloring the subject of the arts and entertainment in Scripture: *music, design, sport, dance, culture, dress, poetry, literature, crafts, color, sculpture, and beauty.*

- The domain of arts and entertainment reveals: *the Potter, our Song*
- The primary attribute of God revealed in arts and entertainment: *beauty*
- God governs this domain through: *the laws of aesthetics of each discipline*
- The color I used: *rose*

WORKING VOCATIONAL MISSION STATEMENT

To provide rest, relaxation, and restoration of the soul through beauty and joy.

A NOTE TO ALL BELIEVERS

One of my students said that he saw how all the domains related to his personal life in one way or another. But not the arts. What did art and beauty have to do with him? He was not a musician or painter or anything like that. I found this a tragic confession. I responded that he needed to ask himself, "Where is the beauty in my life?" Immediately he teared up. The question touched a deep chord. His life was full of service, duty, devotion, and work—but it lacked celebration, beauty, and joy.

This is not uncommon, in or out of Christian circles. The world is desperate for beauty. We are so often surrounded by the mundane, thoughtless, chaotic, and ugly. One of the things I love about living in Switzerland is the celebration of beauty in the form of flower boxes on the windows. No matter how humble the farmhouse, every spring color explodes in all the window boxes. This custom serves no practical purpose. These plants can't be eaten. They are just pretty. There is such a need for this understanding of beauty in all of our lives and communities. Where is the beauty in your life?

My parents were poor and moved from their family homes during the Depression to find work in the northern United States. I was their first child born in a home with an indoor toilet. But from my earliest memory music filled our house. My mother listened to opera on the radio as she washed our hair in the kitchen sink on Saturdays. We never talked about it; there were no music lectures. But it was important to her to have beauty in her very modest home. This is one of my great treasures—the celebration of God in music in my life. We need beauty.

A NOTE TO ARTS AND ENTERTAINMENT PROFESSIONALS

Whether you are gifted in body, ear, or eye, your gift is a celebration of God and a part of the call of God on your life. We have been created by God to need and to celebrate beauty and joy. You are part of God's answer to that world of need. Everything God has made, whether we look at it macroscopically or microscopically, is beautiful. So, whether you are celebrating the use of your gift in the work of the church to minister to Christians or to minister to the many who do not go to church, you are ministering Christ. Whether you work with Christians or non-Christians, you are his testimony through your life and skill. You don't have to justify your gift by creating religious material or by kneeling in prayer when you do well, although you may do both. Your gift is justified because it is part of God's nature and character in you. It is part of who he is and how he has made you, and the gift itself reveals God. The world needs your gift and the celebration of beauty and joy it brings. Do not hold back! Let's begin the new renaissance.

Part III

If We Are Going to Disciple All Nations

INTRODUCTION

The rebuilding of our Christian minds will take time, effort, and the conviction that we cannot fulfill God's vision without it. When I finish writing this volume, I intend to go on to study government from Genesis to Revelation. I pray that you are already preparing for what you will study and apply.

In this third section we will move beyond the domains of society to other areas of thinking that need to be reformed if we are to finish the task of reaching and teaching all nations. This is not an exhaustive list, but it represents the recurring needs I have seen in a decade of teaching this material. To begin with, we will need a bigger picture of who Christ is. Today we love him. The first apostles were stunned by him. Second, we need God to change our concept and definition of nations; otherwise we will fight for the traditions of men rather than the will of God. Third, we need God to restore our understanding of vocation so that we will see our work as an act of worship. Fourth, we must become aware of the ever-present dangers that accompany power and realize that the kingdom strategy is always a servant strategy. Finally, we must embrace, even love and seek, radical change as a lifestyle.

Welcome to the twenty-first century. We have a lot of work to do!

CHAPTER 14

WE NEED A SUPREME CHRIST

If believers are to regain the influence God designed for us in every arena of life, we are going to need a greater revelation of Christ. One of the most important questions in the New Testament, one Jesus was continually leading people to ask, is, "Who is Jesus?" The great transforming truths of the gospel are all contained in the answer to that one question. Who is Jesus Christ?

Like me, you probably feel you have known the answer to that question since you became a Christian. We may say, "Jesus is the Son of God, born of a virgin, and through his death on the cross and the forgiveness of my sin, he is the Savior of my soul." And as far as it goes, that is accurate. With this thinking, we view the gospel as primarily concerned with the "sacred"—things of a spiritual nature, eternal things, heavenly things, things that are holy. We feel we know who Jesus is. But if we separate the secular and the sacred, we will have a very small Jesus. If we are going to regain greater influence as a generation of Christians, we need to wrestle with Jesus' identity, as Paul did in the letter to the Colossians. Let's look at the "size" of Paul's Jesus:

Colossians 1:15–20

He is the image of the invisible God, the firstborn over all creation. For by him all things were created: things in heaven and on earth, visible and invisible, whether thrones or powers or rulers or authorities; all things were created by him and for him. He is before all things, and in him all things hold together. And he is the head of the body, the church; he is the beginning and the firstborn from among the dead, so that in everything he might have the supremacy. For God was pleased to have all his fullness dwell in him, and through him to reconcile to himself all things, whether things on earth or things in heaven, by making peace through his blood, shed on the cross.

What questions were the believers dealing with that Paul is answering in his letter to the church in Colosse? Paul clearly states his desires for the Colossians by saying what he has been praying constantly for them:

Colossians 1:9–14

For this reason, since the day we heard about you, we have not stopped praying for you and asking God to fill you with the knowledge of his will through all spiritual wisdom and understanding. And we pray this in order that you may live a life worthy of the Lord and may please him in every way: bearing fruit in every good work, growing in the knowledge of God, being strengthened with all power according to his glorious might so that you may have great endurance and patience, and joyfully giving thanks to the Father, who has qualified you to share in the inheritance of the saints in the kingdom of light. For he has rescued us from the dominion of darkness and brought us into the kingdom of the Son he loves, in whom we have redemption, the forgiveness of sins.

The Colossians have been converted. They know Christ in a personal way, and they love the Spirit.[1] They have been faithfully pastored in these things by Epaphras, their minister. But Paul desires deeply for them to move beyond these basic foundations of the gospel that have been laid in their lives. He wants them to grow from salvation into knowledge of the will of God, having wisdom and understanding in their daily lives. He wants them to learn what will make them effective in "every good work." He wants them to grow in the knowledge of God so that they may demonstrate through their lives the difference between the "kingdom of light" and the "domain of darkness" from which they have been saved. He wants their "salvation" to get feet and start being walked out in everything they do.

What is important for us here is that the first thing Paul focuses on, in order to accomplish this greater maturing growth in the Colossians' lives, is the answer to the question, "Who is Jesus?" They know him as Savior. They know him as the one who sends the Comforter in the person of the Holy Spirit. But that is not enough! He is more! If they are going to "live a life worthy" of him, they need a greater revelation of his absolute supremacy over everything. Our soul? Yes. Our spirits? Yes. Heaven? Yes. The invisible world? Yes. *And more!* Let's look at how Paul labors with them to understand. How can he spell it out any more clearly?

LORD OF ALL!

Christ created all things. All things in heaven and on earth. He created everything, visible and invisible. All things were created for him, and he ranks as commanding officer of all things. Are you getting the point? Christ is supreme in everything! This means there is no such thing as a "secular" and a "sacred" world. All things belong to Christ. The temporal things of life are not less important than eternal things, because all things belong to Christ. The gospel is not about salvation alone and how Christ saves us. The message is also about God's reconciling power in every area of our lives, families, communities, and nations. What has the cross of Christ, the blood of Jesus, reconciled? Everything! Everything on earth and everything in heaven. Christ has made peace with every part of his creation through Jesus. He is not at war with any part of it. My little brain barely knows how to think about *this* Jesus.

Paul's letter to the Colossians tells us that Jesus is Lord of everything. He is Lord of the so-called spiritual world as well as the material world. He is Lord of salvation and all social concerns. He is supreme over the eternal and the temporal. He is King of heaven and of earth. Because all things were created *by* him and *for* him, they all belong *to* him. He is the rightful heir to all that is, and he has shed his blood to see it all reconciled.

THE MESSAGE IS THE KINGDOM

When we preach salvation alone, we are missing the majority of God's kingdom message. Conversion is essential. There is no other way into the kingdom of God but through belief in Christ. But conversion is the *entry* into the kingdom; it is not the kingdom itself. With our limited gospel we cannot "bear fruit in every good work," because we do not "grow in the knowledge of God" in the rest of life. We cannot be "strengthened with all power," because we do not have the "knowledge of his will through all spiritual wisdom and understanding." Therefore, we are the largest church in history but the weakest church when it comes to influencing the lives, communities, and nations to which we have preached the gospel.

We must destroy the split thinking we have been taught and take up again the gospel of the kingdom. Then, and only then, will not only our words but also our actions and influence bear witness to the absolute supremacy of Christ and his message. How do we do this? How do we restore our Christian minds? How do we get the gospel of the kingdom back?

TWO KINGDOMS

A careful study of the Word of God reveals two kingdoms, or what we would call today, two worldviews. In one view Jesus is Lord of everything, and in the other he is not. In God's view of reality, everything is integrated under his supreme authority. All other religions and philosophies have a split view of reality, where one part of the universe is more real than another. In philosophy this debate uses the language of the one and the many, the ideal versus particulars. Scientists talk about the material versus immaterial, visible versus invisible. In theological language we discuss this dichotomy in terms of temporal versus eternal, earthly versus heavenly. Existentialism puts its emphasis on the unseen world (immeasurable), and communism on the seen (measurable). Hinduism, Buddhism, and Islam say the earthly is unreal—reality is in the unseen world. Empiricism says if I can measure it, it is real. But the God of the Bible says there is no "versus." It all belongs to him. All that has been made is from him and reconciled to him through the shed blood of Jesus Christ. This is what Paul is striving to convey to the Colossians, as is every other New Testament writer to the expanding Gentile and Jewish churches.

The only way we can live in the kingdom of light is by integrating all that comes under the lordship of Jesus Christ. We must remarry the elements of God's kingdom that have been estranged through split thinking. We must dispel the darkness of our minds by refusing the concepts of secular and sacred, the dualism of a lost world. God is not just or merciful. He is just *and* merciful. He is not either the God of heaven or earth. He is the God of heaven *and* earth. God does not care more for the invisible than the visible, the unseen than the seen. He is the Lord of science and prayer. God is not only redeeming his human creation; he is redeeming his material creation. He cares for every bird, animal, and plant he has made. God is not alienated from our ecological concerns; ecology is of vital importance to the Lord who created the earth and everything in it. Christ does not turn a blind eye to earthly justice, preferring heavenly justice. He suffers with those who suffer and calls on his people to give voice to the silenced.

KEYS TO GREATNESS IN THE KINGDOM

In Matthew 5 Jesus reveals the keys to greatness in the kingdom of heaven. He says that we are to integrate the teaching of the Law and the Prophets with his teaching of grace, the cross, and the Holy Spirit, and that "whoever practices and teaches these commands will be called great in the kingdom of heaven."[2]

Matthew 5:17–19

"Do not think that I have come to abolish the Law or the Prophets; I have not come to abolish them but to fulfill them. I tell you the truth, until heaven and earth disappear, not the smallest letter, not the least stroke of a pen, will by any means disappear from the Law until everything is accomplished. Anyone who breaks one of the least of these commandments and teaches others to do the same will be called least in the kingdom of heaven, but whoever practices and teaches these commands will be called great in the kingdom of heaven."

Matthew 13:52

And he said to them, "Therefore every teacher of the law who has been instructed about the kingdom of heaven is like the owner of a house who brings out of his storeroom new treasures as well as old."

If we do not integrate the Old Testament with the New Testament, if we do not preach the old and the new, if we do not integrate the spiritual and material, the heavenly and the earthly, the seen and the unseen, then we are not seeing the real Jesus.

CHAPTER 15

WE NEED GOD'S
VIEW OF NATIONS

Ask of me, and I will make the nations your inheritance, the ends
of the earth your possession.

PSALM 2:8

After this I looked and there before me was a great multitude
that no one could count, from every nation, tribe, people and
language, standing before the throne and in front of the Lamb.
They were wearing white robes and were holding palm branches
in their hands. And they cried out in a loud voice: "Salvation
belongs to our God, who sits on the throne, and to the Lamb."

REVELATION 7:9–10

I f you mark your Bible every time the word *nation* is mentioned,
you will begin to think you are reading a book that is all about
nations. Nations are emphasized at the beginning and at the end
as they all gather before the throne of God. To regain the influence
God desires for the body of Christ on earth, we need God's view of
nations. We must look again at Scripture to see the destiny of the

church in relation to God's whole plan and purpose. What is our destiny here on planet earth? We often pray, "Thy will be done on earth as it is in heaven." What is the will of the Father on earth?

Let's begin by looking at what it is not.

WHAT OUR DESTINY IS NOT

Our Destiny Is Not Only New Birth

God died to save us and desires salvation for all. The only way into the kingdom of God is through Jesus Christ, but conversion is not God's only or ultimate goal for us. The new birth is a means to an end. When we do not preach the whole Word of God, we produce hopelessness. We leave people with a dream of heaven and no sense of their destiny here on earth. When we go to the whole world and preach salvation alone, we neglect the rest of God's plan.

Our Destiny Is Not to Be Filled with the Holy Spirit

God's power in the Holy Spirit is wonderful and essential in the Christian life: God the comforter comes to live within us. We cannot thrive without him. But his filling us with spiritual gifts is not our goal. The tools of the Holy Spirit are a means to an end, not the end in themselves. People who come into the kingdom and go from meeting to meeting to get renewed and filled with the Spirit are cheating themselves. God has more, much more! The coming of the Holy Spirit is part of God's great river that moves us. He is our empowerment to take off—but to where? We must not stop at receiving the gifts of the Spirit; we must go on to use them.

Our Destiny Is Not Miracles

God did create the cosmos. He did part the Red Sea. Jesus did feed four and five thousand with a few fish and a little bread. But each of these miracles teaches us something specific. They are a means to God's end. If we do not understand a miracle's lesson, we are like the disciples in the boat with Jesus.[1] They saw the fish and the bread. They saw the thousands. They held the bread, broke it, and passed it out.

They gathered up the leftovers in huge baskets. They saw, touched, and tasted the miracle food. Then hours later they were in the boat with Jesus and one of them noted that he forgot the bread. Jesus rebuked them, saying, "You of little faith." They had experienced the miracle, but they did not understand what God was teaching them through it. The result was that when they got in the boat, they had nothing—no bread, no understanding. A miracle always points us to something about the nature and character of God and how he wants us to think. Miracles are God's way of preparing us, but for what?

Our Destiny Is Not Churches
Churches are essential to God's plan, but they are not his goal. God's strategy is not to have all his people in church 24/7. God's desire is to use church to prepare his people to carry out their work. But what is the work?

THE ANCIENT MANDATE

For thousands of years God has been trying to reveal our destiny to us. Before the fall, after the fall, and right through the Gospels and the book of Revelation, God is clarifying his will on earth. What purpose has God created us for? In his likeness, as his people, what is our destiny in this life? As we enter this new millennium in his plan, many are still unclear about this.

To Adam, God said, "Be fruitful and increase in number; fill the earth and subdue it."[2] Some translations read "take dominion," others "cultivate the earth." The root word for cultivate is *cultus,* the same root of *culture.* In essence God is saying, "Fill the earth and create tribes, nations, peoples—cultures." To Abraham he says, "I am going to make you as the sand of the sea. I am going to make you as the stars of the sky. I am going to multiply you, and through you I will bless all nations."[3] Multiply! Cultivate! Then through his Son, Jesus, the Father repeats his mandate. Reach every creature.[4] Multiply! Teach all nations.[5] Cultivate! For thousands of years God has repeated our destiny again and again.

Our destiny as the people of God can be summed up in this: Christ revealed in the nations. To understand this, to enter into our full inheritance on earth, we must understand nations from God's perspective. Currently, we understand the need to "reach" the nations. We understand that there is a huge unreached population in the 10/40 Window and that we must target these nations. We understand that we must send workers to tribes and language groups who have no witness. When we see 20 or 50 percent of a population converted and a church planted, we have a tendency to see our work as coming to completion. But this is only the beginning.

GOD'S VIEW OF NATIONS

What is God's view of nations? What is God trying to convey to us in his Word about his purpose for tribes and peoples? To understand God's heart for the nations, we have to start at the beginning—Genesis—and work our way to the end.

Genesis
Before the fall God intended man to fill every corner of the earth and to develop cultures and nations. After the fall the plan continues. In Genesis 10 we begin to see the celebration of nations. You can almost feel God's excitement as he recounts the multiplication of tribes, each with their own language, culture, and land. God loves diversity. He loves multiplication. He loves this massive process of migration and reestablishment of new peoples. God is so pleased with the concept of creating nations that every time someone gets wounded or hurt, he blesses them by promising that he will make them a new people, tribe, and nation.

As God calls Abraham out of his homeland, he promises that he is going to make him the father of a great family of nations. When Ishmael is thrown out of his father's tribe, God says, "Don't worry, Ishmael, I have a blessing for you too." And what is the blessing? "Ishmael, I am going to make you a family of nations. I am going to create twelve great nations through you." Lot is abused in his new homeland, and as he leaves in defeat, God encourages him. "Lot, I am going to make you into two nations." Can you feel the heart of God? God is excited. He is doing what he loves. He is multiplying people in his image and *creating new nations*. When Rebekah is pregnant, God speaks encouragement to her: "You carry two nations in your womb, Rebekah." From God's perspective, being allowed to parent a new nation was an honor. God is using nations to accomplish something dear to his heart. What does he love? He loves people and nations, lots of nations, each with their own language, culture, and land.

In chapter 11 of Genesis we come to the story of the Tower of Babel. I have heard many messages on the sin of the people of Babel, but never one on what appears to me to be the real sin. We often focus on the tower the people wanted to build to heaven and the pride of that aspiration. We see it as using science and technology to exalt themselves over God. But the Tower of Babel is only the symbol of their sin, not the sin itself. What is it in this account that moves God to action? In verse 4 the Babylonians say, "Come, let us build ourselves a city, with a tower that reaches to the heavens, so that we may make a name for ourselves and not be scattered over the face of the whole earth." Babylon wanted to be a "meganation." They wanted to stop the great migration of peoples, gather on a plain in Shinar, and build one great nation with one language, one culture, and one government. They wanted to be the most powerful nation on the face of the earth. God's plan was for multiplication and diversity, and the Babylonians wanted an empire. God defeats their ambitions. They are defeated in their purpose as every empirical dream of domination is defeated in history. God is determined to continue to multiply and create nations.

As God moves on in Genesis from the origins of the cosmos, humanity, family, and nations, he details the origin of one nation. Using Israel as his model, he reveals his plans for human culture. God says to Abraham, "I will teach you, and you will teach the nations."[6] To Isaac God repeats, "I will bless you, and you will bless the nations."[7] To Moses in the wilderness he says, "I will give you understanding of how to be a nation, and through this I will bless all nations."[8] God says that he is choosing Israel because they are a small and undeveloped people. His principles applied will make them the greatest nation on the face of the earth. He can use them to reveal himself in and through all nations. He makes Israel the template of what he wants for all peoples, in all nations, in all of time.

The Prophets

If we look at the biblical prophets, all seventeen of them prophesied to nations. Every one of them had God's word for at least one nation, many of them for more. Today, prophecy is often focused on the individual or the church. This is not wrong, but it was not the focus of the prophets in Scripture. What does it mean that a simple shepherd like Amos had a bigger understanding of God's strategy in nations than we seem to have today?

When we read of the parting of the Red Sea and God's miraculous defeat of the Egyptian army on behalf of Israel, we are not only reading of God's heart for the Jewish nation; we are reading of God's heart for all nations. We are seeing the lengths to which God will go for a people. We are seeing God move heaven and earth in order to preserve his revelation of himself in a people. That is not God's message for *one* nation but *all* nations. He is saying, "I will bless one people so that all nations of the world will be blessed." It is God's desire that every nation be free, have land, and have the right to learn the blessings of God and become examples of the greatness of God.

The Gospels

As we move on to the New Testament, Jesus picks up the thousands-of-years-old theme and says, "Multiply. Disciple all nations." The vision that begins with Adam does not change. God's purpose for all peoples continues through the Good News of righteousness in Jesus Christ. In Matthew Jesus says, "Do not think that I have come to destroy or eliminate the laws of Moses. I have not come to destroy them; I have come to fulfill them. And anyone who does not preach these laws and principles will be the least in the kingdom of God. But anyone who preaches and lives the principles will be great in the kingdom of God."[9] Jesus is saying that the coming of salvation does not eliminate the need to teach and preach the principles of how to live in our communities and how to disciple our nations. We must preach salvation, and we must teach nation-building. When we preach only the New Testament, we are discipling people in being "least in the kingdom." It is good that they are in the kingdom, but God wants more. God desires to release influence and greatness in the kingdom. For this we must return to discipling with the whole Bible.

Recently, I received an e-mail from Argentina. The leaders of the revival there sent out a letter asking forgiveness of the body of Christ worldwide, saying that in their zeal for evangelism and church planting they had failed to address the issues of justice and economics. They felt partly responsible for the national crisis in both these areas. This is a humble response to a devastating fact: we have lost much of God's thinking. We reach the nations, but we leave them in injustice, disease, illiteracy, and poverty. We no longer have the keys of greatness in the kingdom that bring blessing to the community. That is the bad news. The good news is that God wants us to reinherit those keys in our generation.

Paul's Letters

I believe that Paul is the primary author of the New Testament because he understood nations from God's perspective. Some of the apostles wanted Christianity to be a subset of Jewish culture. Paul contested this, saying that the Good News of Christ is not to be a subset of any culture. It is God's message for all nations and is to be expressed in and through their languages and cultures in their own way. If Paul had not won this argument, you and I would be singing Jewish songs and dancing Jewish dances. But Paul did win, and so won the right for the diversity of God to be revealed through all peoples in all times.

Revelation

In Revelation we are given a picture of God's throne and the throng standing before him. How are they gathered? By denominations? No. By families? No. By nations! Nationhood is eternal—it is part of the New Jerusalem. Multiculturalism is celebrated for all time. Nations express the diversity of God and his nature. In the new earth we will come in all our national glory, laying our treasures of justice, health, wisdom, love, beauty, and wealth before God's feet, declaring him the source of all we have that is good. The kings bring the glory of their nations before the throne.[10]

REACHING AND TEACHING THE NATIONS

Nations are miracles. They are birthed by the will of God; they have their origins in the Creator. They cannot exist but by his will. God has made a covenant with every people, and that covenant stands until those people break the covenant. God said to Israel, "You may destroy these nations, but you may not destroy this nation, because I have a covenant with you." God will remove the rights of a nation that has become cancerous, but this is not his desire and purpose. He wants to reach and disciple all nations.

To this day the Jews have failed to understand that their blessing and destiny as a nation lies in the blessing and destiny of all nations. And it seems we as Christians do not understand this either. For God, nations are not targets for evangelism; they are strategies for revealing himself. Nations are not convenient ways for Christians to divide up the work or subheadings to the mission task. God's plan of redemption is for individuals, but it is also a reconciliation plan for nations. Nations were in the heart of God when he created the universe, and nations are there before his throne for all eternity.

God is not after a big church only; he is looking for a diverse church and a deep church. He desires to teach nations and demonstrate the glory of his truth on earth. How do we participate in this? It is all in the Book. Moses' job was to teach the smallest, poorest, most destitute people in history about God and science, God and justice, God and economics, God and family, God and worship, God and wisdom, God and beauty, God and health—in other words, God and all of life. This revelation was learning to think as God thinks and to live as God would live in our place. Moses wrote it all down in the five books of the Law so that the Jewish people, and all peoples of all nations, would have the keys to the blessings of the kingdom.

How do we make great nations for the kingdom of God? We give them the whole counsel of God, and that involves giving counsel to all people in society, no matter their job. Every person has a role to play in God's kingdom.

CHAPTER 16

WE NEED A BIBLICAL
VIEW OF VOCATIONS

For we are God's workmanship, created in Christ Jesus to do
good works, which God prepared in advance for us to do.
EPHESIANS 2:10

God blessed them and said to them, "Be fruitful and increase in
number, fill the earth and subdue it."
GENESIS 1:28

I love to watch children. They are a microcosm of adult social and
physical concerns. They play out life on the surface without inhi-
bition or subtlety. In watching children I often understand others
and myself better. Children know what they love and love what they
are made to do. They will, in a free environment of creativity, play
out their God-given gifts. A coworker told me of his daughter, about
age three, stopping him as he left for work. She admonished that
what he was wearing didn't match. This began a morning routine
that lasted for years of her picking out his clothes. She was good.
Her sense of color, fashion, and flair was all there at the age of three!

Another friend of mine, now the scheduler for a nation's cabinet minister, as a child would create a make-believe desk complete with phone, agenda, and calculator and proceed to make fantasy airline reservations. I used to create a little podium and make speeches to all my friends. From early in life it was clear that my future would involve talking. Children, created in the image of God, know and love what they are created to do.

WORK IS WORSHIP

If we are to reveal the kingdom in all its glory, we need God's perspective on vocation and work. A large part of how we know and enjoy him forever is in fulfilling the work he created us to do. We reveal God, in part, through the work of our hands. Just as God's creation reveals who he is, our work reveals who we are, what we believe, and whom and what we worship. One of the most demeaning experiences for human beings is believing they have nothing to contribute or having their contribution devalued or denied. God gave six days to worship through work and one to rest.

In our focus on evangelism, missions, traditional church ministry, and the secular-versus-sacred dichotomy, we have nearly lost the theology of the laity, a godly perspective of work outside of the institution of the church. When I first came to missions in the early 1970s, we lamented the "funeral services" churches often had for those "laying down their lives" for missions. We thought missionary service was the greatest calling on earth. We thought God had released us into what he had made us to do. Today in ministry circles, we tend to have our own kind of "funeral services" for those poor souls who are going back into "secular" work, just getting a job. Having broken the blindness to the call of God in missions, we in missions developed a new blindness to the call of God to the rest of society.

Tom Marshall, whom I had heard speak in Kona before my "cornfield revelation," estimated that 20 percent of God's people are called to the ecclesiastical work of the church; the other 80 percent are called to serve God's kingdom in other vocations. Over the last century we have devalued work outside the church to the point that much of the body of Christ feels they did not get the "good gifts" like preaching or evangelism. They sit in pews around the world wishing they could really serve God. Our vision for a businessperson is to make money for missions or the church building program. Leaders might serve as church treasurers. Our place for teachers is the Sunday school program. Communicators? Well, we have church newsletters and bulletin boards that need preparing. Artists, musicians, and entertainers are always needed in worship and outreach programs. They might help create worship banners too. Scientists, technicians? Those are tough ones. Fix the church plumbing or buses? Do the engineering for our construction program? Political leaders and lawyers really stretch the imagination for service.

The result of this thinking is that most of God's people go to work five or six days a week to make money and wait for Sunday, when they can do something for God. How tragic! No wonder we are a church that lacks influence. Once we walk outside the doors of the sanctuary, we have no idea what we are to do for the kingdom of God. What we have lost is a theology of work and God's purpose in all giftings. If we are to regain the historic influence of believers in their communities, we will have to regain God's view of all the vocations.

WHO SECULARIZED WHAT?

I want to make a radical proposition. Today, we talk a great deal about secularization in societies—Christmas, Easter, Sundays, and so on. And it is true that much of culture, even religious culture, has been turned into a business venture void of additional meaning. Who is responsible for that secularization process? Many believers think nonbelievers are to blame. But that cannot be true. Such people don't know God and don't have the understanding to change God-centered culture. They do live in a secular world, because their world does not include the living God. Believers, on the other hand, have a choice! We can refuse secularization because God is in the picture. But society is hopelessly secularized when those who know God, when those who are called by his name, take God out of most of life. When we as believers leave God out of our jobs, when we go to work only to make money, then the salt loses all flavor. When the light of the world is dim, it is dark indeed. We as Christians are both the problem and the solution.

GOD'S VIEW OF VOCATIONS

When God created the cosmos, he gave the human race a specific and wonderful part in his design. We are made by God to steward his material world and to create human culture that reveals the full image of God. His mandate in Genesis 1:28 isn't for us to be farmers; it's for us to use our gifts to create, according to his image in each of us. Some of us reveal Jehovah Jireh, God the provider, through our entrepreneurial and business gifts. Some of us, in our passion for justice and service for others, work to serve the community through the justice system. Some of us are compelled by God to make life more beautiful, visually and audibly. Our passion is to reveal the God of beauty. Others who have a passion for truth and knowledge become communicators and educators. Some who long to discover what God has made become scientists and explorers, those who go to the ends of the world, the cosmos, and our reality. Still others have a passion to reveal God the Father by raising future generations to know and enjoy him forever. And others as pastors and teachers desire to help people know God better and worship him with their lives, families, and work. Our gifts are different, but we are all gifted to reveal God in our lives and talents.

REAL CAMEOS

I have the great privilege of traveling God's planet and meeting his people. (Sometimes the thought of getting on one more airplane seems unbearable, but it is never tiring to be in a new culture with a new body of believers.) God's diversity is exhilarating. From all over the world I have cameos of God's people affected by the loss of our vocational revelation.

There is the successful Swedish businessman who wept as we talked about God's call to business. He said that all his life he had somehow known his vision for business was true, but he had never heard it validated by the church.

An English medical student read this material on vocation on my website and wrote to say that she had intended to quit medical school because she deeply wanted to serve God. Now she understood that being a doctor was her service to God.

There is the sanitation engineer who broke down and wept when he heard the vocational mandate of science. He said that no one in the Christian community had ever validated his work to keep his community healthy, whereas his missionary brother was honored every time he visited church with him.

An Indian businessman almost leaped with joy at the good news that business ability was a gift of God. Sadly, some Christians in India have developed a vocation-based caste system in which business is considered the lowest caste.

There is the South African believer who found for the first time that his job of redeveloping old mining compounds into livable communities was a holy calling. He had been assigned millions in tax funds to turn these symbols of injustice and greed—which were partially to blame for the destruction of family structure in the black community—into something that enhanced people's quality of life. He was shocked at how much instruction there was for his job in Scripture.

If we are to become a church of influence, we must embrace God's perspective of all vocational callings! This means a reformation of our thinking about the laity, those called to serve God in the community outside the church structure. We must have God's view of the importance of community and our role as Christians in serving it. Jesus summarizes the whole of the Law and the Prophets into two commandments: "'Love the Lord your God with all your heart and with all your soul and with all your mind.' This is the first and greatest commandment. And the second is like it: 'Love your neighbor as yourself.'"[1] Jesus radically emphasizes God and community as our focus. We need a generation that will become so saturated in the Word of God that they can again articulate God's purpose for every arena of life.

VOCATIONAL MISSIONS MANDATES

The Hippocratic oath, while not Christian in origin, has led the thinking and commitment of medical doctors around the world for more than two thousand years. What might be the result of the world's largest body of believers, the laity, getting a hold of God's thinking on all of work? What would happen if every Christian in the world began to do their work as the call of God and as service to the kingdom? What would happen if, inspired by the Holy Spirit, we began to take an oath to serve the kingdom in justice, in education, in media, in science? Is it possible that the only thing our communities need is for Christians to stop thinking of their work as secular? Is it possible that darkness is really nothing at all but rather the absence of something? What is needed is for the light of believers to shine.

I have a dream. In this vision of the future, I see a generation who can articulate and apply God's view of civil justice, economics, science, education, family, the arts, communication, and church ministry. I see a generation of believers who grow up believing that what they love to do is a gift from God, and who desire with all their hearts to use these talents in the service of God and their community. I dream of young people all over the Christian world taking oaths to serve the kingdom in their specific callings. And yes, I will say it, I dream of a generation who is willing to die for the Lord of justice, provision, and freedom.

After ten years of studying the Scriptures with vocations and community in mind, I believe that every domain has a purpose related to God's identity. Let's look at these vocational missions mandates.

Government: Justice (King of Kings)
To provide an independent and objective source of arbitration and conflict resolution for society and between nations, ensuring justice and equity for all its citizens.

Family: Nurture and Love (The Heavenly Father)
To provide a safe, loving, and nurturing environment for the growth and education of the next generation.

Church: Mercy and Holiness (The Great High Priest)
To spread the faith, to disciple all believers in the whole nature and character of God and in applying his Word to the work and walk of faith, and to facilitate the expression of that faith in worship, fellowship, and the sacraments of the church.

Science and Technology: Order and Power (The Creator)
To discover and use God's natural laws in order to bless all creation by pursuing a higher quality of life, better health, and greater stewardship of God's resources and the created universe.

Economics and Business: Provision (God Our Provider)
To provide needed goods and services and gainful employment opportunities for the community at a fair market price and wage.

Education: Knowledge (The Great Teacher)
To develop the God-given gifts in every person to their highest potential in the service of their community.

Communication and Media: Truth (The Living Word)
To provide truthful, objective information of importance to the community at large so that citizens can make informed decisions.

Arts and Entertainment: Beauty (The Potter, Our Song)
To provide for rest, relaxation, and renewal of the soul through beauty and joy.

This is only a start. We must all work together for God's reformation of a generation and pray, "Thy kingdom come, Lord, on earth as it is in heaven."

CHAPTER 17

WE NEED BIBLICAL STRATEGIES: THE WILDERNESS TEMPTATIONS

No temptation has seized you except what is common to man.
1 CORINTHIANS 10:13

For we do not have a high priest who is unable to sympathize
with our weaknesses, but we have one who has been tempted in
every way just as we are—yet was without sin.
HEBREWS 4:15

If we are to regain Christian influence in our communities, it
is essential that we understand the temptations we face. Jesus
faced three temptations in the wilderness. This event in his life was
important enough that three of the four Gospel writers included it
in their account.[1] For many years I have looked at the three temptations, asking for greater personal revelation of how they apply to
my life. Scripture says that every temptation is common to everyone

and that Jesus suffered them all.[2] Therefore, the biblical emphasis on Christ's temptations is significant for you and me.

THREE TEMPTATIONS, THREE STRATEGIES

In the Matthew 4 account, we are given a setting, a word of temptation from the devil, and the scripture that Jesus uses to counter the attack. Each of the three elements is vital in understanding the text and the temptation. Verse 1 begins with: "Then Jesus was led by the Spirit." This opening shocks me. It plays with my preconceived ideas of what it feels like when the Spirit of God is active in my life. No matter how often I read to the contrary in Scripture, I think that being led by the Spirit will feel great, that it will take me to wonderful places. Matthew says that Jesus was led "into the desert." Into the desert? I thought God's Spirit was supposed to lead us into the Promised Land, into peace, love, joy, and the abundant life. But the Spirit led Jesus into a wilderness. I don't like it, but that is what God's Word says. The Holy Spirit's purpose in taking Jesus there was "to be tempted by the devil." Jesus was not tempted because Satan had it in for him. He was not tempted because he had sin in his life. God led Jesus into purposeful, strategic temptation to prepare him for the call on his life. The devil was involved, but God was the active agent in this situation.

Verse 2 says, "After fasting forty days and forty nights." After! When Jesus is hungry, weak, isolated, and vulnerable in every way, that is when the attack comes. The Spirit of God has led him to fast, led him to the wilderness, led him to vulnerability, and then allows, even initiates, the accuser of his soul to come at that moment. This tests our understanding of the character and ways of God. Even though we say his strength is proved in our weakness, we still think attacks will come when we are strong.

Matthew goes on in verse 2 to say, "He was hungry." The simple, infuriating humanity of Jesus rebukes us when we want to be more than human. It stares back at us when we would have the world see us as invincible and strong. The sheer human need he suffered humiliates our desire to have no needs.

TEMPTATION ONE: IDENTITY IN THE FACE OF PHYSICAL NEED

In this setting of severe and abject physical need in the wilderness, "The tempter came to him and said, 'If you are the Son of God, tell these stones to become bread'" (v. 3). Be careful here. What is the temptation? Can God turn stones into bread? Of course. That does not tempt the power of God. Does God want to provide for his children? Yes! Does he care about their basic physical needs? Of course. A loving father does not give a stone when a child asks for bread. Neither God's power nor his love for his children is being tested here. It is something much more subtle. Something far more human.

The key here is the word *if*. "*If* you are the Son of God. . . ." Jesus is being tempted to doubt his identity. In the face of desperate physical need, when Jesus does not have what every human being must have to survive, the devil says, "*If* you are the Son of God. . . ." Meaning, "Are you the Son of God? You hungry, thirsty, bag of bones, heap of filth. Really? You are the beloved Messiah, full of power? You? If you are, prove it! Do a little miracle for me. Demonstrate a little of that galactic power. Feed yourself. Produce a little miracle bread—*if* you can." Later in Jesus' ministry, at least two of his public miracles involve creating miraculous amounts of bread. But that is not the test of the moment. The temptation here is to doubt who he is in God, to doubt his Sonship, his inheritance, his acceptability to the Father in the face of physical need. That is the first test.

Jesus does not fall for this subtle test of his identity. He responds, "It is written, 'Man does not live on bread alone . . .'" (v. 4). Jesus does not deny that he is hungry. He does not deny that he, like every other man, needs bread. He does not fall into debate over God's ability or willingness to provide what is needed. He simply acknowledges that bread is not our only need. And he goes on to quote more scripture: "'but on every word that comes from the mouth of God'" (v. 4). Every word! Not just *some* of God's truths but all of them, including God's word recorded just four verses earlier: "This is my Son, whom I love; with him I am well pleased."[3] The word had been spoken through the prophets, the angels, the wise men, Elizabeth, Mary, Joseph, and then a voice from heaven. Jesus would not doubt the truth of these words just because he was facing physical need. The enemy is defeated by Christ standing on the truth of his Father's words about who he is.

TEMPTATION TWO: IDENTITY AND THE NEED TO DEMONSTRATE SPIRITUAL AUTHORITY

Round two! A new setting. The devil takes Jesus to the holy city and stands him on the highest point of the temple. How did he do that? Was it a vision? Was it transport of the kind Philip experienced in Acts 8:39–40? We don't know. Jesus is experiencing a manifestation of some sort. He was in one place, the wilderness, and now he is on the pinnacle of the temple. What a heady sensation that must have been. What an adrenaline rush. The setting has been transformed now from one of physical need to one of spiritual heights. Satan has taken him to the center of religion, the greatest of earthly spiritual symbols.

Here Satan says, "If you are the Son of God . . ." (v. 6). The same words. Is it the same temptation? Yes! But this setting is no longer in the context of physical need and weakness. Now Jesus is in the midst of spiritual exaltation. He is high and lifted up, looking down on his holy city from the pinnacle of the temple, tempted to doubt his identity in the Father, tempted to doubt that he is the Son, and if he does believe that he is the Son, tempted to prove it. This is his chance to demonstrate to everyone's satisfaction who he is. He can show them now.

This is a powerful temptation. If you have ever served in ministry, you have experienced this temptation. Somehow you have been raised to a place of prominence, a place of being *seen* by others in ministry. On one hand, you experience joy that you can serve God in this way. You have a genuine desire to use this exposure to help people. But there is always something else stirring inside, an inner dialogue that prods, challenges, and nags. "How did you get here? Do you really think God can use you? Others probably think you are a fool. Do you have any abilities? Prove it! Do something spectacular." The temptation is to attempt to prove yourself powerful in ministry. Subtly, but surely, the temptation moves us from focusing on the Father to focusing on proving our spiritual authority. We begin to need to pray "bigger" prayers, preach more amazing sermons, see more miracles. Soon, the need to see the spectacular becomes the focus. The emphasis is drawn away from the Father and simple, secure obedience to his will to our performance and the need to prove we are his heirs.

At this point on top of the temple, Satan challenges Jesus to throw himself off the temple, and he gives him a "scriptural" reason: "For it is written, 'He will command his angels concerning you'" (v. 6). Whenever we are tempted in the spiritual/religious arena of life, Satan will help us along with a scripture of his choosing. He helps us justify our insecurity by making us believe we are really doing something for God. *This is really not about proving my spirituality,* we think. *This is giving God the chance to prove himself.* But that is the point—God does not need to prove himself.

Now Jesus responds with his own scripture: "It is also written: 'Do not put the Lord your God to the test.'" Jesus knew that he was not on earth to defend his Father but to obey him, carry out his will, and demonstrate who the Father is. It was not his role to create difficult circumstances for God to then prove his power or faithfulness. Jesus was not here to test and prove God but to serve him.

The first two temptations of Jesus are basic and common to anyone called to follow Jesus. In insecurity we begin to doubt what the Father has already said is true—that we are accepted as heirs of his kingdom. When we doubt that position, the enemy moves us into striving for demonstrable proof. "If you are a child of God, heal that baby, heal your body, see that money come in. If you are an heir of

God's kingdom, take this risk, do this impossible thing, prove this scripture," the enemy taunts. The key to discovering the enemy's devices is not found in questioning God's ability to do any given thing we might ask; the key is in the word *if.* "If you are the Son of God. . . ." It is an identity question. Who are you? And if Satan discovers that we do not accept or grasp that God embraces us as his heirs, that we are acceptable in his sight because of his grace, then Satan has found fertile ground for temptation and deception.

Jesus knew who he was. When the Father spoke at his baptism, "This is my Son, whom I love; with him I am well pleased," Jesus believed him. For the Son of God, the identity question was settled. Seeing this, Satan moves on to the next temptation.

TEMPTATION THREE: RIGHT IDENTITY, RIGHT VISION, WRONG STRATEGY!

Round three is a shift in the enemy's strategy. When Satan discovers one temptation is not working in our life, he will try another. "Again, the devil took him to a very high mountain and showed him all the kingdoms of the world and their splendor" (v. 8). This is a very different setting. First, Satan tempted Jesus through physical hunger and need. Then he tempted him with religious desires. And now with the nations. This reminds me of the picture that John describes in Revelation where Jesus, restored to his throne, has the glory of all the nations paraded before him.[4]

Satan shows Jesus a vision. Jesus sees all the nations in all their splendor. What a sight that must have been. The enemy must have thought that this surely would lure the Son of God. Here is the strange thing: the nations and all their splendor already belong to Jesus. They are his rightful inheritance, and the Father has assured him they are his. So what is the temptation? What is Satan offering? This is not an identity question; Jesus knows he is the Son of God. This is not a question of misguided direction; the nations and their splendor are his. Wanting the riches of the nations and the power that they represented was not Christ's temptation. What then is the temptation? The essence of this temptation is found in these words: "All this I will give you . . . if you will bow down and worship me" (v. 9). It is the wrong method!

The enemy says, "All right! You know who you are. You know you don't need to prove it, and you know what belongs to you. I will make you a better offer than the Father. I will give you the nations—now!" No waiting, no ridicule, no opposition, no trial, no jail, no beating, no cross, no death. Jesus can go straight from the quiet life of a carpenter to ruler of the universe. All he has to do to simplify the cost of obtaining his vision is change his allegiance from the Father's method to Satan's method. "Bow down and worship me," Satan says. Whom will Jesus obey?

Jesus is unwilling to be swayed, and he rebukes his enemy by name for the first time. "Away from me, Satan! For it is written: 'Worship the Lord your God, and serve him only'" (v. 10). Jesus clearly identifies who is speaking when the tempter proposes a shift in allegiance and a painless, fast, and easy road to power. Jesus knows he is dealing with Satan himself.

CONCLUSION

What can we learn from this important time in Jesus' life as we contemplate our desire to disciple the nations? First, we know that identity will be a struggle for the body of Christ. Who are we to talk about building nations in the face of such physical need, hunger, poverty, and disease? Or, on the other hand, who are we *not* to accomplish great things? Haven't we worked hard to establish our ministries? Both of these attitudes need correcting in light of our true identity in God.

Second, we will experience the subtlest of all temptations—the fast, painless, power strategy to inherit the goal. Is it possible that at strategic moments in church history this temptation has delayed God's purposes in the nations? Did the crusaders grasp their identity in Christ and the vision of the nations but pollute God's purposes by bowing to a power methodology? Did they embrace the vision of

God but the strategy of the enemy, the sword rather than the servant heart of Jesus? As we look over the historical landscape of the church and the mandate to disciple all nations, it seems possible that this last temptation has been our greatest hindrance.

I worked in Washington, DC, for several years. Christian groups were coming en masse with a renewed vision for discipling America. The "power" of this capital city was and is tangible. As new people arrived in the city, the environment began to work on them. Whether they were politicians, activists, or lobbyists, Christian or not, they showed a dramatic shift in objectives from "national service" to "national power." I saw few who were able to resist the temptation.

As we will see in the next chapter, the Bible offers a different model of power and influence. God uses slaves and servants to influence nations.

CHAPTER 18

WE NEED BIBLICAL
STRATEGIES: THE
SERVANT MODEL

Whoever wants to become great among you must be your servant, and whoever wants to be first must be your slave—just as
the Son of Man did not come to be served, but to serve, and to
give his life as a ransom for many.
MATTHEW 20:26–28

If we are going to disciple our communities, we need a fresh revelation from God on the power of serving. The word *servant* and
its derivatives take up nearly five pages of listings in my NIV con-
cordance. The men and women God used for great influence in the
kingdom were seldom people of status and power. Noah, a farmer.
Abraham, an old man with a barren wife. Joseph, the despised youngest son of herders. Moses, a person raised in power and splendor but
not of great use to God until he had lived for forty years as an outcast and fugitive in the desert. David, the son no one remembered,
a family outcast. Esther, a destitute orphan with no social status or

means. Ruth, a widowed refugee with a penniless mother-in-law. Nehemiah, a slave-servant to a pagan king. Daniel, an exiled boy with no means or freedom.

The pattern continues in the New Testament as the Son of God comes to us not as the king of the cosmos in all his splendor and glory, but as a lowly carpenter in a modest family from an insignificant village. Jesus chose ordinary, working-class men to lay the foundation of the church. And the architect of evangelism, Paul, a man of great means, status, and education, is reduced to a servant of all before he is used to build the kingdom.

What are we to understand from this consistent scriptural theme? What is God's perspective of power that makes the humanly powerless more influential than those with great worldly status? What is this preference Jesus has for using the smallest, the youngest, the poorest, and the most disenfranchised? What does God know about power that we are still missing?

A STRATEGY OF SATURATION

The pastor of a West African president (who himself desired to see his poverty-stricken nation discipled by the Word of God) asked me an incredibly insightful question. As we discussed national strategy for the country, he said, "If you had to choose, which would be your priority—to target the leaders of vocations in our country, or to target the churches and the pastors as a strategy of national reformation?" I looked at him with great respect, because so few know enough about the kingdom to realize how key this question is. This man had done his homework with God.

I responded that I would rather not choose, that I believed that God would build his kingdom in every direction given the opportunity. But he prevailed in this fictional scenario, and for discussion's sake I had to choose. My response was unequivocal then. I would choose a grassroots, local-church saturation scenario for national change.

Gandhi is noted to have said that the British would rule India as long as the Indian people wanted them to. By sheer force of numbers a people united in anything will overrule the power of a few at the top. The few can only be the majority influence as long as the many do not care or remain silent.

In Genesis 1 God gives the human race his pre-fall mandate: "Be fruitful and increase in number; fill the earth and subdue it." This mandate was not for one man, Adam, to have authority over everything else, but for all of God's human creation to saturate the earth with the knowledge of God revealed though all dimensions of everyday life. The kingdom of God is a saturation strategy.

This is dramatically demonstrated in God's exhortation for Israel not to choose a king but rather a more grassroots system of tribal leaders and representation. Though God reasons with Israel through the prophet Samuel, they choose a king anyway.[1] God works with them in their choice to make the best of it. As Israel grows in strength politically and economically, it begins to appear that God has either made a mistake or reversed his opinion on power. Under Solomon's rule, Israel reaches a pinnacle of national development. Surely this strategy of a king is blessed. The ark is returned. The temple is built. They have peace on their borders. The economy is booming. The law is revered in the palace. What could be better?

Did God make a mistake? Was it better to have a king? The answer to that question is just one king away: Rehoboam. In one generation, one rotten egg spoils the pot. Rehoboam turns against God and destroys three hundred years of development that Israel never again achieves. When only the kings knew the law, the people could be led anywhere. The only protection for a nation is a people saturated with the knowledge of God and embracing responsibility.

Gandhi had a profoundly biblical point to make about power: it resides in the people. The quality of the people will ultimately determine the quality of a nation. The top levels of society can be godly or pagan, but the people determine how long their influence will last and how deep it will go. The top echelons of society can open and close doors. They can institutionalize values and principles that outlive them, but ultimately the saturation of those values and principles into everyday life will determine the quality of the culture.

THE KINGDOM IS WITHIN YOU

Both the Old and the New Testaments emphasize this internalized quality of the kingdom. It is *living* the kingdom, *being* the kingdom that will ultimately accomplish God's mandate. In Deuteronomy, Moses passionately exhorts the people that God's law is not far from them; they don't have to send messengers to bring it back from across the sea or the heavens.[2] The Law is with them. It is their knowing and practicing of the Law that matters. The kings should know and read the Law, yes, but emphasized even more is that parents know the Law and constantly teach their children to integrate it into their daily lives.

Jesus reduces all of the Law to two sentences that capture the whole: "'Love the Lord your God with all your heart and with all your soul and with all your mind.' This is the first and the greatest commandment. And the second is like it: 'Love your neighbor as yourself.'"[3] This deeply personal summation embodies God's strategy. We are to be the kingdom. We are to live the kingdom. The salt and light of our lives will "salt" and "light" the earth with the knowledge of God. You and I are God's strategy. Discipleship, or learning to apply God's thinking to our daily lives, is God's focus.

As I began to realize this personally, I longed to live in a neighborhood to understand how this worked itself out practically. I had discipled students and leaders in their professions for years, and I would continue to do so. But what did the neighbor mandate look like? I bought a home in the southern part of the United States on a street of fourteen houses. I chose a multiethnic street, because God loves the nations. I got a little house because I am single and travel extensively; God is a good steward of resources. I began to work on my yard (which had been neglected for at least a decade), because God loves beauty and we are to care for the material things he gives us. In the first few weeks my neighbors would watch me as they worked in their yards. I would wave and keep on trimming, raking, hauling. After a time, some started to come by when they saw me out working. They would say how nice the house looked and ask my name. We'd talk gardening for a few minutes and they'd be gone. I would go in the house and write my neighbors' names down so I would remember, because God knows our names. After more time our "yard conversations" would get past the weather and the trees to what I do. Finding out I was a missionary didn't lead to much discussion, because it was so foreign to them, but we continued to get to know each other through the things we had in common: houses, yards, plants, neighborhood safety, and so on.

As I worked on my home, I prayed for my neighbors, their families, our neighborhood. About six months after I moved in, one neighbor made a beeline for me one morning. He said, "Please pray for my wife. Her sister just died." Within a week another neighbor saw me in my yard, made a direct path to me, and said, "My wife said her job is more important than me, and I'm afraid I'm going to lose her. Please pray." I was astounded. We had never spoken of prayer. We had hardly said anything about God. My neighbors knew I was in ministry overseas, but I had not shared many details. Where did this desire for God come from, this trust with the most intimate pain in their lives? I can only believe it was the testimony of my yard work and neighborly concern. They saw Jesus in the care of my house, in the desire to know and remember each of their names, in the willingness to be "one of them" first, and in the shared concern for all of our homes, families, and safety. They saw Jesus in my life, and they wanted more of him in their crises.

OUR LIVES ARE THE MESSAGE

One of my early influences in the kingdom used to say that in the Christian faith *you* are the message. In that sense biblical faith is not a religion or a set of ideas to talk about without application to our lives. Following Jesus is a way of life, a relationship with God that turns into the kingdom lived out on a daily basis. I fear that for many, following Jesus has become a religion, an ideal we can talk about believing without it necessarily changing any dimension of our lifestyle. Faith becomes about salvation and life after death, and there are parentheses around the rest of existence as though God has nothing to do with it.

It is interesting that Christians have no difficulty talking about *how* Jesus would have lived as a carpenter those first thirty years. They know that he would have been timely in his work; he would have treated his workers and customers respectfully and cared for them as people; he would have paid his bills on time. We understand that if Jesus made a bookshelf, the shelves would be straight, the construction sturdy, and it would be beautiful, even if simple. He loved quality. Jesus would have taken good care of his tools, and he would not have wasted wood and other materials. There is this innate understanding in all of us that he would have been generous with his income, mowed his lawn if he had one, and that his house would have been clean. Jesus' personal hygiene would have been exemplary. And, if we push our thinking a little harder, we know why Jesus would have lived like this—because of who his Father was.

The testimony of Jesus' personal life for thirty years in Nazareth was the authority base of his three years of ministry. If we cannot serve our family with the principles of the kingdom, if we cannot serve our neighbors with the principles of the kingdom, then how can we serve the nations with those principles? But, going a step further, if every Christian in the world were living his or her personal life by the principles of the kingdom, would not the nations be discipled?

SERVICE, NOT CONTROL

The system of the world is based on power: let's take over and make it better. The kingdom of God is based on service. Had it been better for Jesus to come with earthly trappings of power, he would have. If control from the top worked, Eastern Europe would still be communist. Leaders may bring about change, but ultimately, if a nation is not changed on an individual level, the nation will not be discipled. God's values may be written into the civil statutes of a nation, and that will have an effect. But if the culture is to be changed, those same values must also be written on the hearts of the people.

In the last half century we have begun to think that we can help create democratic nations through military action from outside forces. We certainly can change a regime by force. However, changing the hearts and minds of the people is another matter. The thinking that created the problem cannot fix the problem. To influence our world we must first understand God's perspective on how it has changed in the past and how it will change in the future.

CHAPTER 19

WE NEED A GODLY PERSPECTIVE ON CHANGE

You know how to interpret the appearance of the sky, but you cannot interpret the signs of the times.
MATTHEW 16:3

Men of Issachar, who understood the times and knew what Israel should do. . . .
1 CHRONICLES 12:32

If we are going to have influence in the nations, we must be people, like the men of Issachar, who know the signs of our times.

As we discussed in chapter 8, the church once held that the earth was the center of the universe. The scientists who challenged this idea were treated harshly. They were not only viewed as wrong scientifically but were deemed heretical for challenging God's Word and authority. However, the scientists were on the right track to discovering more about the solar system and the universe.

The God who created all and knows all is not shaken when our limited understanding goes through a learning curve. His supreme desire is that we ever grow to be more like him. As the old hymn declares, "He is changing me." He is also changing our view of his creation. God is not in conflict with truth, with facts, or any reality of the seen or unseen world, and he is not afraid of change.

In our age it seems everything is changing constantly. It is estimated that the average person will change professions four or five times in his or her lifetime. Engineers today find that half their professional knowledge is obsolete every five years. Graduates today have been exposed to more information in one year than their grandparents were in a lifetime. Ninety percent of the information and knowledge required for jobs over the next five years has yet to be invented. Mind boggling, isn't it? To us perhaps, but not to God.

God is not experiencing a knowledge surge. He has had all this in his grasp from the beginning. We have nothing to fear from information and knowledge, old or new. Facts can only reveal God, his nature, and his ways.[1] But, as finite human beings, we do fear change and always have.

FEAR NOT!

Imagine yourself as an Israelite in Moses' day. For four hundred years your people have been slaves to the pharaohs. In the last few months you have left Egypt and all that is known to you. You are in the middle of a desert; you have no known source of food and water; you cannot go back to Egypt; you have no idea what is ahead in this unseen Promised Land. You are experiencing a paradigm change of all you know, and God must remind you time and time again, "Fear not, for I am with you."

Today, we experience that kind of shaking change again and again. In a world daily attuned by microchips, global economics, space telescopes, and instant information, our sense of reality can get shaky. When our reality begins to unravel, we feel insecure, and often insecurity results in rigidity and a desire to control. When we shut down and refuse to understand the changes in our world, we stop growing. The fruit of all this fear is that we miss God's expanding revelation of himself through the universe he created.

Esther came to understand that God had a plan for her nation in the crisis in her life. She realized that her uncle Mordecai's words were true: "Who knows but that you have come to royal position for such a time as this?"[2] The pressures and changes of her day were purposeful for the kingdom of God. She was afraid, but she turned to God in her fear and saw change work for his glory in her people.

In this day of global upheaval and what feels like disaster and doom, we need an Uncle Mordecai to tell us that our times are purposeful. For, if God tarries and the end of the world is not at hand, we may live in a century of the greatest influence on the world for God's kingdom in the history of the human race. Let's get God's perspective on our times.

GLOBAL SOCIAL REVOLUTION

One simple way of looking at the evolution of human societies and cultures is to see it in three primary cycles: the tribal or feudal system, the great city-states, and our more modern concept of nations.

The Tribal or Feudal System

Nearly all of human society was at one time organized around something resembling a tribe. Whether the leaders were patriarchs, chiefs, or landlords, communities were organized and defined around the availability and ownership of land. In Scripture the tribal age extends from Abraham through the era of the judges of Israel. Until King Saul, Israel was a consortium of twelve tribal groups loosely networked through the leadership of a judge.

In medieval Europe this was called the feudal system. The head of this socioeconomic system was the lord. The lord owned the land, and the peasants worked it. The lord provided any education, health care, or law. In practice, a farm or a farm-based village defined citizenship and community. Itinerant priests traveled from farm to farm. The lord recruited, trained, and equipped the military. Early European monarchs depended on the benevolent support of the lords' armies. Today, many African and Middle Eastern nations are still tribal underneath the veneer of more modern social structures.

The Great City-States
As population-driven cultural evolution took its course, the world's communities were transformed. The next period of social structure was characterized by the development of the great city-states such as Rome, Athens, Alexandria, Constantinople, Babylon, Hamburg, and Paris. These cosmopolitan centers functioned like the later developed nations. One was a citizen of Rome. Rome built the roads, was the seat of education, controlled the economy. Taxes were collected and paid to Rome. This was the world of Paul's day. Paul held dual citizenship in Rome and in Jerusalem, which he found useful in his work for the kingdom.

Populations continued to grow and finally outgrew the politico-economic infrastructure of city-states. Rome and systems like it became incapable of meeting the needs of their constituents. The world began to turn itself over once again as city-states gave way to nations.

Modern Nations
Today, we speak of Italy with a city called Rome, of Greece with a city called Athens. We understand that Hamburg is in Germany and Constantinople is in Turkey, Alexandria in Egypt and Paris in France. Geopolitical borders have been created and changed again and again to form the world we understand in our time. When we are asked where we are from internationally, we name our nation first, even if our nation still has tribes. We carry national passports and discuss national economies and educational systems. We sing national anthems and fly national flags. We have national constitutions and governments and tend to see our culture as defined by national tastes and values.

This is our modern understanding of nations, but this was not the concept of nations when God spoke to Abraham about making him a nation. Nor was it the concept when Jesus told us to go to all nations. And yet all of Scripture is telling us to address the needs of and disciple all nations.

HERE WE GO AGAIN!

Population is again driving change in our geopolitical structures and economies. Increasingly today, with nearly zero population growth in Europe, a bursting population in Asia, and inadequate population-to-resources equations in other regions, our world is once again evolving in how we define ourselves. National economies are failing or becoming unstable. National militaries are finding themselves inadequate to protect. National education systems do not prepare a generation for the global community in which we live. For the fourth time in human history, society and nations as we know them are reinventing themselves.

Europe leads the way in this with the formation of the European Union. It's not that the French, German, English, Spanish, and others do not love their nations, cultures, languages, and even currencies. They do. But their systems no longer work for the populations in our world today. They must redesign themselves to fit the reality of the twenty-first century. And Europe is not alone. As the European Union takes shape, one hears discussions of "the Americas," with new treaties and economic dialogue between North and South America. A new term appears in our vocabulary, "Australasia." We see new collaboration and coordination in the Middle East and identify it as the "Arab World." We talk of global economies, regional stability, multinational forces, and even world courts.

In the face of this dramatic shift, many people panic, forgetting that it has all happened before. Some begin to focus on a one-world government and the end of the world instead of understanding that every major shift in history has moved us in that direction. But the church's job remains the same: disciple all nations. History can give us a more positive understanding of global change and the times we live in. We are not the first generation of believers to face global shifts in social systems. And, if God tarries, we may not be the last.

CHANGE IS GOD'S CATALYST

Change is not always cataclysmic, but it is always a catalyst. History teaches us at least three wonderful truths about change:

1. Whatever God meant by nations in Genesis, he intended his truth to be applicable to all times and all nations, regardless of change.
2. Throughout history, great change has provided the best climate for influence.
3. The church has, in some measure, found its voice and brought God's truth to influence each major shift in our global history.

In this century when, by God's grace, we have the largest population of believers worldwide in human history, and we are in what could be one of the greatest centuries of change in the history of the planet, will the body of Christ have a voice? In an age of change, Calvin gave us a concept of public education, Wilberforce pushed for just labor practices and laws, Carey for economic development; others founded the Red Cross, developed a code of ethics for treating prisoners of war, rules of war, scientific research, laws of evidence, and the list can go on. These things took place when men and women of God understood that we can't control change, but we can use it. We can steer change toward the values and principles of God.

All over the world, leaders are scrambling to find new definitions of just war, just rules of war, legal combatants, protocol of prisons, labor laws for women and children, women's rights, the rights of multicultural populations, religious freedom, the poor versus the rich, the power of governance, balance of powers, and national versus international issues. We are panicked with the sheer volume and totality of change we see. God is not! None of these issues are new; they have all been dealt with before. God dealt with them in discipling Israel, and his dealings come complete with a record of the values that are not negotiable if we want quality of life and with volumes of case studies of success and failure.

What if the largest church in history linked up with the greatest community-building values in history to bring the greatest kingdom revolution in history?

LET THE NATIONS BE TRANSFORMED

Who's to say when the end of the world will come? For two thousand years believers have thought it would be in their lifetime, including the apostles who walked with Jesus. But it was not in their lifetime, or century, or millennium. The end of the world as we know it will come. Yet Jesus tells us not to focus on that but rather to be salt and light in our time and to work until he comes.

We may be living in the greatest century in church history, *if* we

- grasp the whole revelation of God in the whole Bible;
- understand God's commitment to the whole community and to all nations;
- overcome our fear of change and embrace these times as the greatest for potential kingdom impact;
- stop staring at the influence of evil and give ourselves wholeheartedly to the influence of good.

If we had focused on discipling the nations in the last 150 years instead of simply evangelizing them, much of Southern Africa, South America, and Asia would be transformed.

They still can be! What are we waiting for?

Appendix 1:
The Bible—God's Big Picture

For an entire year I studied the Bible from the standpoint of God's purposes in it. Making the assumptions that God inspired each book of the Bible and that the church fathers were inspired in ordering these same books, and believing that it is no small miracle that the church has basically agreed on these things for two thousand years, I then asked: what was God's strategy and emphasis in the books chosen and the order in which they are placed? This was a mind-blowing study! The following is a summary of the contents of the Bible.

THE BOOKS OF MOSES

First, we have the five books of Moses, the template of Hebrew thought.

- **Genesis:** The origins of the cosmos; of the individual, family, tribe, and nation; and of sin.
- **Exodus:** Israel's current events from God's perspective and what God is doing with Israel as a community in space and time.
- **Leviticus:** The formation and workings of the priesthood and the tabernacle.
- **Numbers:** The logistics of discipling these people into a nation.
- **Deuteronomy:** The overview of how God wanted Israel to live in every area of life.

These five books, called the Pentateuch or Torah (Law), laid the foundation for all of the Old Testament and, as we will see, for the New Testament as well.

NARRATIVE BOOKS

All the other books in the Old Testament refer back to the first five. They evaluate the history and forecast the future of Israel based on what God has laid down in the Law. The rest of the Old Testament relays events and history based on the answer to one simple question: Are we living up to God's principles in the first five books?

Let's look at what God emphasizes in the books following the Pentateuch.

- **Joshua** (Community/Government): How they do in the Promised Land in the first generation of political action.
- **Judges** (Community/Government): How the next thirteen generations of judges (rulers) do in the political arena.
- **Ruth** (Individual/Family): After seven books emphasizing communities and nations, God narrows in on two powerless and poor women who are blessed when they obey in faithfulness.
- **1 and 2 Samuel, 1 and 2 Kings, and 1 and 2 Chronicles** (Community/Government): The history of the political leaders and how they did or didn't obey God's law.

That makes eight books for government, one for family, one for the priesthood, twelve books for community, and one for the individual. Seeing any pattern yet?

The next books, Ezra, Nehemiah, and Esther, are a trilogy. They are not in order. Esther is actually first chronologically, Ezra second, and Nehemiah third. They are all exiles in the capitol city of Sousa. In about 479 BC Esther marries King Xerxes and as a result is used by God to save the lives of all the Jewish people in exile. In about 456 BC, twenty-one years after Esther's story, Ezra, a priest, returns to Jerusalem and rebuilds the temple. The city is still in chaos and disrepair. He is there thirteen years, without success in restoring the community, when a letter reaches Nehemiah, part of the king's palace security guard, telling of the disasters in Jerusalem. Nehemiah is sent by the king with supplies and support to rebuild the wall and restore order and infrastructure to the community. So we have:

- **Ezra:** Community/Priesthood
- **Nehemiah:** Community/Government
- **Esther:** Community/Family and Government

Esther saves the people. Ezra restores the temple and the Law, and Nehemiah rebuilds the government and community economic system—all areas emphasized by God as essential parts of kingdom life.

Our count is now government ten, family two, ecclesiastical order two, community fifteen, and individual one.

WISDOM LITERATURE

We love the wisdom literature, I believe, because each book focuses on the individual. These books deal with dimensions of the believer's personal life. What is important in our daily lives? Worship, wisdom, work, family? All of them!

- **Job:** Individual and Family
- **Psalms:** Individual and Worship
- **Proverbs:** Individual and Wisdom
- **Ecclesiastes:** Individual and Work
- **Song of Songs:** Individual and the Wedding (Family)

What is Job doing here? Job is the oldest book of the Bible to the best of our understanding. He was, perhaps, a contemporary of Abraham. I think most of us see the wisdom of the church fathers in not selecting Job as the first book of the Bible. Its theme of suffering and personal warfare is tough stuff even for the most mature believer.

Job is the second book in the Scriptures to look at the story of an individual without it being particularly important to the history of the community. Like Ruth, Job is important because of his walk of faith and obedience to God under great duress. Job begins with great power but is reduced to nothing by a series of attacks and disasters. After seventeen books focusing on the principles by which God has made the universe to work, the blessing of knowing and applying these truths to our lives, and the curse of not obeying them, God introduces quite a different focus in Job. For the first time since Genesis, God tells us that there are additional challenges to obedience. We have an enemy, and even if we make all the right choices, there may be another explanation for difficult circumstances in our life. We may be experiencing Satan's attack! Today, many people seem to have reversed this emphasis to everything being a spiritual attack and almost nothing the result of our choices.

That brings us to ten books focused on government, three on family, six on the individual, and two on the priesthood or ecclesiastical order.

THE PROPHETS

Then we come to the seventeen prophets. Some authors of these books were priests, some were shepherds, some government officials. All the prophets speak to nations or communities as a whole. They all emphasize the cause-and-effect nature of our choices and the resulting blessing or curse. Each prophet focuses on four major areas of sin no matter what nations they are addressing.

- Idolatry: ecclesiastical order
- Political justice: government
- Immorality: family and individual
- Economic injustice: business and finance

God's emphasis on the importance of the ecclesiastical institution (church), government, the individual, and the family is overwhelming. The focus on the community is almost unanimous, and the emphasis on knowing God's thinking and aligning ourselves with it in how we live is complete. The revelation of the values and principles of the kingdom are written. Now, where do we get the power to live it?

THE NEW TESTAMENT

What do we see in the New Testament? Each Gospel writer emphasizes a different source of authenticity in portraying who Jesus is.

- **Matthew** defends Jesus as the Messiah by drawing heavily from Old Testament sources (*ecclesiastical history*).
- **Mark** emphasizes Jesus' relationship with the material world and his power over it (*science*).
- **Luke** takes the view of an investigator, looking at the testimony of those who were with Jesus (*legal*).
- **John** uses the personal, eyewitness account of the *individual*.

The Gospels, like the books of Moses, lay a foundation for the lordship of Christ. Moses lays a holistic basis for God's rule over all of creation and life; the apostles lay the same foundation for the lordship of Christ.

Now we come to the book of **Acts,** which I think could be called The Explosion! The word about Christ bursts out from the new church and explodes with conversions, gifts of the Holy Spirit, healing, miracles, persecution, public proclamation in Jerusalem and beyond, and the establishing of the church internationally. The "explosion" begins with the new converts accused of being drunk and ends with some of them in jail. What a roller coaster.

In the books that follow, we begin to see and deal with some of the issues within this new international church movement. The gospel travels out of Jewish territory and begins to encounter the surrounding worldviews, and a shift in emphasis occurs among the Jews as well.

- **Romans** asks the question, "What are we going to do with the Old Testament?"
- **First Corinthians** takes up the question of how the Holy Spirit works.
- **Second Corinthians** asks where the authority of this new church comes from.

The next nineteen letters reveal a pattern of themes not dissimilar to the Old Testament. In various circumstances, nations, churches, and individual lives, we begin to deal with the drift hazards of the new church. Here are some of the major themes of these letters:

1. What do we do with the Old Testament and the laws of Moses?
2. What is the function of the Holy Spirit?
3. Where does authority come from in this new church?
4. How do you/we know you/we have authority?
5. What are the conditions for elders and deacons and the character qualifications of a church leader?
6. How do we discern false teachings from true ones?
7. How do we live? What is our position on family, immorality, government, finances, honesty, work, and generosity?
8. What is the nature of eternity and life after death?
9. What perspective do we have on persecution and endurance?
10. What do we believe about the supremacy and return of Christ?
11. What do we know about the end of time?

You can almost feel the struggle of the New Testament leaders trying to integrate the Old and the New Testaments, grasping the Spirit and letting go of the Law, or grasping the Law and letting go of the Spirit. Throughout all these discussions, Christ is presented as the only way to salvation, the Law and the prophets as the teachers of how we should live, and the Spirit as the one who leads us into applying the principles of the Law in daily life. Nowhere do we see one discarded in preference of the other. All of the letters are full of tension from integrating the old covenant with the new covenant.

THE LAW AND THE GOSPEL

Matthew, I believe, is the first Gospel for a reason. Matthew makes an all-out effort to link Jesus with the Old Testament. At least forty-nine times in twenty-eight chapters, Matthew links the life and teaching of Jesus with Moses and the prophets. In Matthew 5:17–19 Jesus makes his position clear on the place of the Law.

> Do not think that I have come to abolish the Law or the Prophets; I have not come to abolish them but to fulfill them. I tell you the truth, until heaven and earth disappear, not the smallest letter, not the least stroke of a pen, will by any means disappear from the Law until everything is accomplished. Anyone who breaks one of the least of these commandments and teaches others to do the same will be called least in the kingdom of heaven, but whoever practices and teaches these commands will be called great in the kingdom of heaven.

This is such an amazing passage. Jesus makes it clear that the new messages of forgiveness and salvation on their own are not adequate for discipleship, but rather build on the foundation of the Law and the prophets. In Matthew 13:52 Jesus says every teacher of religious law who has become a disciple in the kingdom of heaven is like a person who brings out of the storehouse the new teaching as well as the old. In Matthew 5:19 Jesus exhorts that the teaching of the new without the foundations of the old will produce weakness and the "least" in the kingdom, but combining the two will produce greatness in the kingdom of God. Mark 7:8–13 accuses the Pharisees of substituting God's laws with their own traditions. And in Luke 16:16–17 Jesus challenges the crowds that by preaching the good news of the kingdom he does not mean that the Law has lost its force; the Law is stronger and more lasting than the universe itself.

After Jesus clarifies the place of the Law and the prophets in Matthew 5, he goes on to give six examples of how he builds his teaching on the teaching of Moses.

1. Murder: Jesus affirms the commandment "You shall not murder," but he goes further to build on that law. He says now that the Spirit is coming, the people should not even act in anger. In fact, they should go a step further and be reconciled before they come to worship. In other words, they are not to murder, and because they are saved and forgiven, their standard will be even higher.

2. Adultery: Jesus affirms Moses' teaching not to commit adultery, but he challenges the people to have an even higher standard of a pure heart.

3. Divorce: Moses taught the people that divorce must be legally carried out, but Jesus tells them that divorce must be under the direst circumstances or it is equal to adultery.

4. Being truthful: Moses taught them not to break an oath; Jesus goes a step further to say that they are not to break a promise or a verbal commitment.

5. Righteous vengeance: Moses taught that they should only seek righteous vengeance, but Jesus says to give up the right to personal vengeance altogether.

6. Loving your neighbor: Moses encouraged them to love their neighbor; Jesus says do that and go much further—love your enemy.

In the face of a world lost in sin, Jesus lived out the principles of God in daily life, in the context of his family, work, and community. Less than 10 percent of his life was spent in direct ministry and open proclamation of the gospel. He spent ten times more of his life living it out. His authority in ministry was in part the authority of his life in applying Moses and the prophets to his times.

CONCLUSION: THE WHOLE BIBLE
AND WHOLE KINGDOM

What happens when we remove the foundational principles of the Old Testament from our discipleship of new Christians? Is it possible that we produce a Rwanda where a church with sixty-plus years of constant revival can participate in tribal genocide? Is it possible that we produce an American church where recent Gallup Polls say there is no measurable difference between the lifestyle of the Christian population and that of the non-Christian? Is it possible that this is the reason divorce in the Bible Belt now exceeds the divorce rate in the rest of America? Can this be why the average Christian businessman in Korea is no more committed to his word in a contract than the average non-Christian businessman? Could this be why in 80-percent-converted Nagaland, 70 percent of the teens in the capital are reported to be drug addicts? Is it possible that this is why modern Christianity makes no measurable difference in the landscape of the societies that surround us? Are we preaching a gospel that, because it is not grounded in the Old Testament teachings, is producing the "least in the kingdom of heaven"?

When we preach what the apostles call the "milk" of the gospel—salvation, repentance, heaven and hell, and the forgiveness of sin—without the "meat" of how Christ expects us to live, we are in danger of producing a new mysticism, a religious belief detached from any physical reality in life.[1] We develop a faith that requires no change in thinking or lifestyle, that is unattached to the cause-and-effect relationship of our choices and the laws of God. Yet we are called to "take captive every thought."[2] We are to be transformed by the renewing of our minds.[3] How can we do this if we have not laid the same foundations Jesus laid? Jesus was discipled by the Old Testament. Paul was discipled by the Old Testament. We do not understand their thinking if we are not interpreting the New in light of the Old.

In many cultures the most important indicator of what kind of person you are and of your value is how you relate to your neighbor.

This was also part of the Hebrew view of the world emphasized throughout Scripture and in the teaching of Jesus. Jesus stressed this community perspective by putting our love of God alongside our being a good neighbor. If I love God, I will love my neighbor. In Luke 10 Jesus is talking to a religious expert who attempts to get a limited definition of neighbor. He asks, "And who is my neighbor?" (v. 29). In response to this Jesus tells the story of the Good Samaritan. He changes the definition of neighbor from "those who live close to me" to the one who crosses your path and who is in need. In other words, anyone, everyone.

What happens when the church switches the biblical emphasis from our responsibility to our neighbor to personal holiness? I believe we create the new monasticism, a spiritual pursuit of God that is completely alienated from social responsibility and action. We create the concept that my personal holiness is independent from how I interact with the community God has placed me in. I can love God and have almost nothing to do with the people living around me; I can have national truth without national responsibility; I can seek to live with only those who believe as I do so that my life will not be sullied with the messy lives of non-Christians. Our walk with God is evaluated strictly on personal merits, not from our participation in the life of our community.

Years ago I was sponsored by a concerned Christian to attend a political fund-raiser in California. My benefactor thought I might be able to get to know and influence some of the county officials. At the time, this area was one of the most Christianized communities in America. I spent time with a local county judge, a single woman about my age. She was very honest and forthright, so I asked her why she did what she did, knowing that she had a tough job and couldn't be motivated by the money or the hours. She said that, at the end of the day, she did it to help children at risk. She had great authority as a judge to intervene in their lives at points where it could make a big difference.

I asked her what part of the local community she found most open to bringing these children into homes. She knew that I was a

Christian and seemed reluctant to answer until I encouraged her I was not thin-skinned—I wanted an honest observation. She said, "Well, it is not the Christians who want these children." She had found the greatest openness to be among the Jehovah's Witnesses and the Mormons. The great revivals of this country in the 1970s may have produced the first megachurches, the first contemporary Christian music, the first of a new breed of Christian bookstore, but they have still not touched the community.

Similarly, former President Mbeki of South Africa was quoted as saying that he would be behind any effort to help change the Christian community's lack of social concern. While the ruling political party is majority Christian, it is the Muslim minority who seem to have the energy and drive to transform South Africa.

Let's bring back the whole kingdom with the whole Bible and the supremacy of Christ in all things!

APPENDIX 2:
THINGS I AM NOT SAYING

My study and research for this material has been almost entirely from the Scriptures themselves. In the very beginning of my search I felt the Lord say that I was to leave aside reformation history and books on the domains. This has worked very well for two reasons. The first is that I teach the material straight from the Bible rather than from history. This means that as I travel the nations, there is no cultural or historical bias from outside sources. I am not teaching some country's interpretation of history but the Word God left for all nations, for all times. The benefit of that cannot be over emphasized. Secondly, it allows me to be both appreciative and critical of the church fathers: appreciative of the great revelations they did have in their nations in their times and the way that influenced history, but also critical of what they were missing from Scripture that would have made them even more influential. This is certainly not the only way to study, but it has proved most beneficial for me.

As I have spoken on these issues worldwide, I have become more aware of the many great conflicts in the body of Christ around concepts like the kingdom, dominion, and discipling nations. I am constantly faced with tough questions that come from a particular view not contained in Scripture itself. I am not qualified to speak to any of these views, as I have not studied them. But I would like to clarify what I am saying by telling you what I am not saying. For some of you this will be a waste of time; for others it may be the thing that helps you hear my message without interpreting it through a different viewpoint.

1. I am not saying that we can create heaven here on earth.

We cannot create perfection here on earth. Only when Jesus returns and a new heaven and new earth are established will we see him in his full glory. However, we can reveal him in part and improve our communities by living out and working for God's values in all of life.

2. I am not saying that Jesus will come back once we disciple all the nations.

Only the Father knows when Jesus will return. The date is never to be our concern; we are always to be prepared. Our job is to obey Christ and, as Luke 19:13 says, occupy or take dominion until he comes. When we put these together—our occupancy and Christ's imminent return—we develop a sense of urgency that works against discipleship, which takes time.

3. I am not saying that Christians are to "take over" society and tell everyone else what to do and how to live.

We will not eliminate sin in our world by discipling communities. However, with evangelism and discipleship we will make better communities. This, in turn, reveals God in a broader way and enables more evangelism and discipleship, which can create even better communities. But we will always have the lost and the saved who are undiscipled, and they will continue to make choices that are less than godly. We are not looking for control; we are looking for influence. The way of the kingdom is not by force but by persuasion. We are salt and light, not a hammer and sickle.

4. I am not saying that God died and left us here to do the best we can.

Jesus is very much alive and active in our efforts. We can glean the principles from Scripture with faithful study and prayer. But we cannot possibly know how to apply these principles to our nations and our times without fresh revelation in time and space from the Holy Spirit. We are not alone with God's manual; he is with us in applying the Word.

5. I am not saying we should do everything like the English, the Americans, the Swiss, the Dutch, or whatever your nationality may be.

A great temptation in teaching and working with this material is to choose a particular national application as the reference rather than sticking with God's examples in Scripture. When we focus on a particular nation, our listeners immediately think of all that nation's faults and our point is lost. There is no "discipled nation," and there is no nation that does not have elements of God's principles in practice. God's goal is not for us to copy one another but to seek a dynamic equivalency of kingdom principles in our community, in our time, and in our way. God loves variety. We can learn from everyone. We should seek to emulate only God, not one another.

NOTES

1. WHAT'S WRONG WITH THIS PICTURE?

1. Frank Newport, "This Christmas, 78% of Americans Identify as Christian," Gallup, December 24, 2009, http://www.gallup.com/poll/124793/this-christmas-78-americans-identify-christian.aspx.
2. Matthew 6:10 KJV.

2. WE'VE LOST OUR CHRISTIAN MINDS

1. Michael Cassidy, *The Passing Summer: A South African Pilgrimage in the Politics of Love* (London: Hodder & Stoughton, 1989).
2. George Kinoti, *Hope for Africa and What the Christian Can Do* (Nairobi, Kenya: AISRED, 1994), 1.

3. WE'VE LOST OUR MISSION

1. John 17:4.
2. Joshua Project defines "the unreached" as those peoples "among which there is no indigenous community of believing Christians with adequate numbers and resources to evangelize" their group (http://www.joshua project.net/definitions.php).
3. Kinoti, *Hope for Africa*, v.
4. Nehemiah 1:3–4.

4. THE CORNFIELD REVELATION

1. Exodus 12:37–38.
2. Genesis 46:26–27.
3. Exodus 1:6–7.
4. Exodus 12:40.
5. Deuteronomy 4:5–8.

6. GOVERNMENT

1. Romans 13:6–7.
2. 1 Samuel 8.
3. 1 Samuel 10:1; 1 Samuel 16:13; 1 Kings 1:34.

4. 1 Samuel 10:24; 2 Samuel 2:4; 2 Samuel 5:1–3; 1 Kings 1:39–40.
5. 2 Samuel 4.
6. 2 Samuel 5:1–5.
7. Numbers 14:6–9.
8. 2 Samuel 5:1.
9. Matthew 12:25.

7. ECONOMICS

1. 2 Thessalonians 3:10.
2. Kinoti, *Hope for Africa*, 12.
3. Genesis 12:3; 18:18; 22:18; 26:4; 28:14.
4. As we can see in 2011, America, having given up on God's financial values, is experiencing commensurate downturn.

8. SCIENCE AND TECHNOLOGY

1. 1 Kings 4:33; Psalm 104.
2. Romans 1:20.
3. Colossians 1:16.
4. Leviticus 12:1–5.
5. Numbers 31:19–24.
6. Numbers 19:16.
7. Numbers 19:11.
8. Leviticus 15:19, 25.
9. Leviticus 15:2, 16.
10. Leviticus 15:7–8.
11. Leviticus 15:4, 9.
12. Deuteronomy 23:10.
13. Leviticus 5:3.
14. Leviticus 7:21.
15. Leviticus 15:20–21.
16. Leviticus 13:2–3.
17. Leviticus 13:59.
18. Numbers 19:7.
19. In South Africa, "one in three women aged 20 to 34 years is HIV-positive, as is one in four men aged 25 to 49 years" (UNAIDS, *Outlook Report 2010*, 77).
20. Kinoti, *Hope for Africa*, 7.
21. Isaiah 53:5.
22. 2 Corinthians 12:8.
23. Kinoti, *Hope for Africa*, 3.

9. CHURCH

1. Numbers 3:12.
2. Numbers 3:12; 18:6–7.

3. Numbers 7:9.
4. Numbers 18:21, 24; 35:2–3; Deuteronomy 18:1; Joshua 14:4.
5. Numbers 18:20; Deuteronomy 12:12; Joshua 14:4.
6. Leviticus 13 and 14.
7. 1 Samuel 9:16; 10:1.
8. 1 Samuel 11:15.
9. See 1 Chronicles 15:2.
10. Numbers 4:15; Deuteronomy 10:8.
11. 1 Kings 8:1–4.
12. Matthew 21:12–13; Mark 11:15–17; Luke 19:45–46.

10. FAMILY

1. "New Marriage and Divorce Statistics Released," Barna Group, March 31, 2008, http://www.barna.org/family-kids-articles/42-new-marriage-and -divorce-statistics-released.
2. Deuteronomy 6:7, 9.
3. 1 Timothy 5:8.
4. Matthew 23:23.
5. Exodus 21:24; Leviticus 24:20.
6. Genesis 4:23–24.
7. Leviticus 19:18.
8. Luke 10:27.
9. James 2:8–9.
10. Judges 4:8–9.
11. 1 Corinthians 13:4–7.

11. EDUCATION

1. Romans 12:2; 2 Corinthians 10:5.
2. 1 Corinthians 14:15.
3. Acts 4:32.
4. Romans 8:6.
5. Luke 2:46–47.
6. 2 Corinthians 10:3–5.
7. Bruce Olson, *Bruchko* (Seattle: YWAM Publishing, 2005).

12. COMMUNICATION

1. 1 Corinthians 9:22.
2. Mark 3:11–12.
3. Mark 3:11; Luke 4:34.

13. ARTS AND ENTERTAINMENT

1. Exodus 15:2; Isaiah 64:8.
2. Deuteronomy 32:44.
3. Exodus 31.

14. WE NEED A SUPREME CHRIST
1. Colossians 1:4–8.
2. Matthew 5:19.

15. WE NEED GOD'S VIEW OF NATIONS
1. Matthew 16:5–12.
2. Genesis 1:28.
3. Genesis 22:17–18, my paraphrase.
4. Mark 16:15.
5. Luke 24:47.
6. See Genesis 12:3; 18:18.
7. See Genesis 26:3–5.
8. See Deuteronomy 4:5–6.
9. Matthew 5:17–19, my paraphrase.
10. Revelation 7:4–10; 21:24.

16. WE NEED A BIBLICAL VIEW OF VOCATIONS
1. Matthew 22:37–39.

17. WE NEED BIBLICAL STRATEGIES: THE WILDERNESS TEMPTATIONS
1. Matthew 4:1–11; Mark 1:12–13; Luke 4:1–13.
2. 1 Corinthians 10:13; Hebrews 2:18; 4:15.
3. Matthew 3:17.
4. Revelation 7:9; 21:26.

18. WE NEED BIBLICAL STRATEGIES: THE SERVANT MODEL
1. 1 Samuel 8:19–22.
2. Deuteronomy 30:11–14.
3. Matthew 22:37–40.

19. WE NEED A GODLY PERSPECTIVE ON CHANGE
1. Romans 1:20.
2. Esther 4:14.

APPENDIX 1: THE BIBLE—GOD'S BIG PICTURE
1. 1 Corinthians 3:2; Hebrews 5:12–14.
2. 2 Corinthians 10:5.
3. Romans 12:2.

Bibliography and Resources

Cahill, Thomas. *How the Irish Saved Civilization: The Untold Story of Ireland's Heroic Role from the Fall of Rome to the Rise of Medieval Europe*. New York: Nan A. Talese, Doubleday, 1995.

Cassidy, Michael. *The Passing Summer: A South African Pilgrimage in the Politics of Love*. London: Hodder & Stoughton, 1989.

Kinoti, George. *Hope for Africa and What the Christian Can Do*. Nairobi, Kenya: African Institute for Scientific Research and Development, 1994.

Miller, Darrow L. *Discipling Nations: The Power of Truth to Transform Cultures*. Seattle: YWAM Publishing, 2001.

Olson, Bruce. *Bruchko*. Carol Stream, Ill.: Creation House, 1978.

Mattson, Ralph, and Arthur Miller. *Finding a Job You Can Love*. Nashville: Nelson, 1982.

Schaeffer, Francis A. *Genesis in Space and Time: The Flow of Biblical History*. Downers Grove, Ill.: InterVarsity Press, 1972.

Stott, John. *Involvement: Being a Responsible Christian in a Non-Christian Society*. Old Tappan, N.J.: F. H. Revell, 1985.

Stott, John. *Issues Facing Christians Today.* 4th ed. Grand Rapids: Zondervan, 2006.

Sheldon, Charles M. *In His Steps.* Grand Rapids: Chosen, 1984.

WEBSITES

The London Institute for Contemporary Christianity
www.licc.org.uk

Relationships Foundation
www.relationshipsfoundation.org

Jubilee 2000 Online
www.jubilee2000uk.org

Professor Prabdu Guptara, Switzerland
www.prabhu.guptara.net

Vishal Mangalwadi
www.revelationmovement.com

About the Author

Landa Cope is the founding international dean of the College of Communication for Youth With A Mission's University of the Nations. She has a bachelor's degree in art and education and a master's degree in humanities and international studies. Since joining Youth With A Mission (YWAM) in 1971, her public speaking and work in missions have taken her to more than 110 nations. Landa currently lives in South Africa and serves as executive director of The Template Institute.

THE TEMPLATE INSTITUTE
AT THE UNIVERSITY OF THE NATIONS

Founded in 2005 by Landa Cope, The Template Institute (TTI) is committed to a comprehensive biblical approach to issues in the public forum. The goal of TTI is to reveal Christ in all of life and enhance the effectiveness of professionals in all spheres to meet the needs of their communities through their vocations.

Working from the Books of Moses through to Revelation, TTI is dedicated to understand Scripture applied to daily life and work.

The structure of TTI is an independent institute seeking to create a training bridge between the professional community, Youth With A Mission (YWAM), and the University of the Nations (UofN). TTI is part of the family of ministries of YWAM.

The target audience of TTI is Christian professionals in the marketplace and professionals of all persuasions with an interest in the biblical foundations for nation building.

Strategies include:

- authoring The Old Testament Template series
- publishing
- Web resources
- virtual and real-time seminars and conferences
- book, video, and audio resources
- forums dealing with critical issues in the public domain
- biblical foundations for positions and values

For further information, events, and resources,
please visit: www.templateinstitute.com